Trans
Ta

2 In The Beginning God Unveiled
6 Who Am I
10 Be With Me
13 Let us Be Known
17 Remember Me
19 Oceans of Apathy
22 My First Love Forgotten
25 The Righteous Restore
30 Seekers Cry God's Reply
34 Finding Grace (Ruth)
38 Caught in His Grace
40 Transformed to His Way
43 Enlarge my Heart
45 Call Me to Another
48 Refuge in thy Wandering
53 Rest In Me
56 Psalms 86
59 I Dare You
60 Much of The Least of things
64 Rebuilding The Temple
67 Redemption is Coming
71 Beloved a letter From God
74 A Call None will Chase
76 To Die is Gain
79 Meet On The Mount
84 How long will You Stand?
88 Stand Fast in Liberty
92 I am a Helpless One
97 House of Grace
101 I am Here
103 Rebuild Your Temple
106 Reflections
109 Unlock Your Mind
112 Woe is Me
117 Keep What has Been Committed
123 Faith Standing in The Power

124 Faith and The Song
127 Where Would I be
128 Why Does the Heathen Rage?
130 Move Me
134 Harps in the Willows
136 A Sweet Savour
138 The God that Holds My Hand
141 Return to The Landmark
143 Preach
145 There is One
147 Growth in Trial Strength in Storms
149 I Seek not Yours
151 I Suffer
153 A Precious Stone
155 Roots of righteousness
156 Is There Not a Cause
159 I must Decrease

In the Beginning: God Unveiled

In the Beginning, Your eternal plan unfurled.
A perfect creation had fallen, Your redemption is
coming for the world.
Your Holy heel destined to trample
the serpent's head.
An eternal promise, A nation with a lineage chosen
for a messiah to be bred.
Always faithful to us as Abraham's promised Son is
received.
Even when in our doubt we chased our own
provision as we were deceived.
The world of evil is judged by an immersing flood.
There is still your promise of redemption in Your
son's shed blood.
A Holy nation is called out from an empty womb.
A holy savior coming to die and leave an empty
tomb.
In the beginning eternal God our Savior from the
start.
A creator of great power, creator of the heavens
yet desires to have my feeble heart.
A cherished relationship with man, although we are
nothing more than dust
A fallen creation that when given the choice follows
after our many lusts.
A lust for power, a lust for knowledge we should
have never known.
The only knowledge we needed was the relationship

we had with You Lord on Your throne.
In the middle of Your presence why did we ever choose to leave?
Separated from it now, it is Your word that we now long for and seek to receive.
Separated from You oh God how great the distance and how great the darkness in my soul.
Lord God speak to me again for it was Your words that made me whole.
How were we proclaimed to be good, when in Your foreknowledge You saw our plight?
How can be there be perfection out of dust and acceptance in Your sight?
Can You hear our cries wishing to turn back time's clock.
I now walk with a broken body and can do nothing more than build You an altar upon a rock.
Wrestling You oh God for nothing short of a vain blessing Your covenant stands strong, I encounter Your glory and fall on my knees confessing.
But Instead of judgment, You give me a new name.
A name that identifies me as Yours with a message to proclaim.
Amidst all my failing you establish a covenant of love
A covenant incomprehensible, a covenant sent from above.
Before the garden, before the flood, before the oppression of sin.
God of All, Yahweh, Elohim, determined in His heart to redeem the world we are in.

In Grace you began all things as Your breath of life was put into me.

Now a living soul in a frame of dust I am given a world to rule and live free.

Guilt had no place, although by my choices my dominion has been taken away.

In Grace You called out my name and clothed me, promising a new way.

You are God, able to do what I cannot.

In faith will I follow your voice, sacrificing the things that for so long I sought.

For You know my heart, my devotion to you and my intent.

Although wavering in step, I will follow You oh Lord and sacrifice the provision you have sent.

For upon this altar Your love will be on display.

For there is an altar to come that Your Son will be sacrificed and save me from the evil way.

To think I am part of Your story, part of a lineage that brings forth the coming Messiah and eternal king.

A nation as stars in the sky and as the sand of the sea.

Using the feeble, the weak and the outcast of civilization from such a man as I comes a people, Holy, Sanctified and Your chosen nation.

From Your word I know now that what is meant for evil, can in the end be turned to good.

For You direct my path and have me live in the way that I truly should.

I will never understand although you are gracious to give me vision of promise and great aspirations.

To see my life used as a blessing among all in spite the a brother's evil imagination.

From a pit, to a prison, to a seat of power above all You promote the righteous through trials and lift us up when we fall.

How tender Your mercy, how precious is Your word. Soften my heart in my troubles so Your voice can be heard.

From the start You are God that has loved, provided and has never failed.

In the beginning Grace was made manifest and our God is unveiled.

Who Am I?

Who am I God that you consider me one to heed
to what you have to say?
Who am I to be counted as one of your children
when with your children I did not stay?
Who am I, I ask because I do not know where I
stand?
Who am I to be your messenger or to carry out Your
commands?
I have been blessed in my past, and a living miracle
among the others now meek and humbled.
But I am not the one to talk as my lips are slow and
prone to stumble.
I stand on your Holy ground, but I am evil and
ordinary to the bone.
I am not set apart from the rest as I am a murderer in
the wilderness reaping what I have sown.
I try to appease others, and do great things so they
may be free.
But everything I touch Lord is cursed and I can only
corrupt everything I see.
Consume me in Your fire, burn me to the dust.
For I am nothing more than what this world can offer
where moth can corrupt and the air will rust.
Who am I, I cannot ask You anymore as I stand on a
my experience and a solid case?
But your presence refuses to leave me and continues
to stay in this hallowed place.
I am with you, I am with you that is all You say as You
respond to my plea.

I am with You... go to the world and set my people free.

"I am God, I know exactly who you are.
You are the one I am choosing right now to lead my people to be as countless as the stars.
You are what I will define you to be, nothing that you can ever prescribe.
You will be what my character imputes to you and what I will describe.
You are my prophet, my messenger, my sanctified saint.
You are not anything apart from me other than a man covered in sin's taint.
So who are you today, now that You stand before Your Holy God?
What question is this, when I have been with you from your conception and saving you from Satan's rod?
Leave Egypt with my people, their stay has come to an end.
For I have heard the cry of my people and it is my word I now send.
I will display my glory before you and the entire world for a time and season.
So go let my people free and know the suffering to come has great purpose and reason.
For the longer the suffering the greater my redemption.
The greater the persecution, the greater will my name be when it is mentioned.

The longer the suffering, the greater your
depravity in your soul will be made known.
And the greater my salvation from above from your
Almighty God seated on grace's throne.
For I am not just leading you out of Egypt or its
oppression, I am leading you to me where there is
purity and perfection.
I will give my law; I will demonstrate who you are
before my face.
No matter what provision I send, you will fail and fall
short without my grace.
You will learn that you are cursed, but in me you are
greatly blessed.
You will see my glory, and you will be tried in the
wilderness.
For who you are cannot be described here in this life
Who you are is in me, so I send you out to keep my
promise, and bring forth my Son fitted for your strife
Who you are is not from this earth, but is defined
and was ordained from above.
Who you are now is a fallen creature, but in me I will
redeem you to be a living vessel of grace and love.
Who you are is not what you have done or what I will
have you do.
Who you are is not a question anymore as I am with
you.
For my name will be written on your forehead,
my nature will be yours to hold.
Your glory will be as my Son's glory with the light of I
AM with wisdom and truth untold.
Who you are is not your purpose, but it is mine.

For who you are is defined by my Grace and love divine.

Your flesh and soul constrain you, but they do not and cannot define or designate what I have in store for you, my chosen sons and daughters. Let my life be in you and resonate.

Let Who I am be who you are.

Be the apple of my eye and the redeemed morning star.

More glorious than the host above that is what I intend you to be.

Perfect by sacrificial love, eternally dwelling with me.

You are my pearl of greatest price that I gave all of myself to receive.

You are my treasure and my glory, a channel for my love to be shed abroad.

Who am I but your Savior, your sacrificial provision upon the cross?

The one who greatly loved you and was willing to give it all for all that was lost.

For no greater love is this, than a man lay down his life for his friend.

This love have I given you, and my life have I given so that our friendship may never end.

May who I am be the Holy ground on which you forever stand.

For love I did not spare and victory on the cross I have saved you from Egypt's oppressive hand."

Be with Me: Be Holy for I am Holy

Be with me I hear a call within my Heart.
Be with me, The God of Israel, part of the Holy
nation, eternally set apart.
Enter into my courts, past the brazen altar, into the
Holy place. Walk past the veil, as a purified priest
meet me face to face.
The things I think of you, the many things I wish to
say. If you would come near and be with me, you
would Not have to wander and stray.
For in Your heart is a wilderness like the one my
precious Sons and daughters travailed.
One that was entered in salvation but persisted in
disobedience with seas of doubts endlessly sailed.
Taste and see my glory it is my desire to have you
before me now.
If you saw the value of the wilderness, you would not
doubt my faithfulness and the strength I endow.
For in the wilderness, just like my children in history I
prepare you for war.
For a Holy one in a broken world must learn to fight
and take on challenges like never before.
To take on the impurities of life and combat the lies
of perverted truth.
Dwell in my Holy presence before the promise,
dwell in the booth.
For in the wilderness in this booth, I desire not for
you to stay. There is a promised land within your
heart that is made for you, but I am its only way.

Purify yourself by the sacrificial blood, send away the
scapegoat, and accept the sacrificial lamb.
For in blood is the essence of life and life is
what is required to satisfy the great I Am.
Eat the clean things of my word for it is your health.
Do not eat of the uncleanness of the world with its
many vanities and wealth.
Keep your heart for out of it are the issues of life.
Be purified in the wilderness; build a tabernacle to
bring before me your sin and strife.
For in the law, you will see there is a perfect and
complete path.
But by grace are you saved, you are free from
the wages of sin and my wrath.
Let grace reign in your heart's wilderness, it will
permit you to walk acceptable and sanctified.
Be with me in grace, a consecrated Priest, a Prophet,
and an anointed king eternally justified.
Keep the Holy feast, remember what I have done.
Remember the incarnate Savior, the perfect sacrifice
on the Cross, the resurrected Son.
Remember these things in your heart, for great
wickedness and lies will impose.
The promises of God will keep you pure and will lift
you past the thorns as a brilliant rose.
If you ever flee from me, I have built a place of safety
and refuge where your sin will not be on display.
Be with me within my refuge and consequence of sin
will not find you as long as I stay.
For I am the Most Holy Priest eternally standing at
the gates.

And I am making intercession for you my precious
sons and daughters saving you from sin's harsh fates.
Bring me your sacrifice, your life of sin, death, and
despair. Give unto me your sinful desires,
your lust, and denial for Me to repair.
Be with me, set the tabernacle, as a great temple
within your heart.
Have for me an altar, a secret place where I set you
apart.
Be Holy for I am Holy, Be perfect as my Father in
heaven is perfect, let this be the triumph of Grace.
For in your heart, there is a wilderness, a tabernacle,
a promised land, and a Holy place.
⏹

Let us be Known: The Numbers

Number the people, number your might count all
that has been given in prosperity and in plight.
Each generation accounted for, every family
member, genealogy and name.
I, Your God, will stand greater no matter how great
your number, or how vast you became.
Number all of your flock, but not to boast in what
you have done; not to boast in your victories or the
battles you have won.
You will boast in one thing as you number and
wander this sea of sand.
The boasting will be in Yahweh, Elohim, Adonai as
your life is within His merciful hand.
For you were not chosen out of Egypt out of tenure
or notoriety.
You were not a famed people, a people of riches or a
people with wisdoms of great variety.
Remember you were chosen of the least, although
great you have become.
Remember the glory you have now is the gift of the
Most Glorious One.
You have not received favor out of works of the law
or by the trials you have overcome or defeated.
You have received favor by grace from the Godof
grace on the highest throne eternally seated.
How great your number, how great you have
flourished and multiplied.
Do not forget Oh Israel, Saint of God, these are
things God has supplied.

For when we number great we can soon be
overcome and fall.
For pride comes into our hearts and separates
us from the God who freely gave us it all.
Devising schemes against authority of which God has
ordained; for a season of seven days your soul will
be outcast and sin stained.
But the season has come to an end and God's Grace
stands strong. Be Restored into the fold of the
Chosen rejoicing with praise and song.
Our numbers become great as pride and
murmuring poisons our heart.
Lord spare this generation, as You have spared me,
purify us and give us a clean start.

We fail once again; in rebellion the world swallows
us whole.
Lord, cover us in your grace and restore our lost
souls.
Restore a Holy priesthood as our attempt to keep it
was vain and corrupt.
Save us continually from the mind of evil, quell the
rebellion within before it erupts.
Our number has decreased, as we suffer great loss
from our sin. Raise the Brazen serpent high in our
hearts, so we may see the hope and redemption.
We are commanded and greatly loved by the Lord
Most High. I pray that we speak and fellowship with
You, Oh Lord draw us nigh.
As we draw closer, we are prepared for the promise,
for the eternal dwelling place.

We have forfeited Your Holy Law in ourselves; accept us in Your Son's grace.

Number your people, number your might,
The call from our Savior comes again may we be acceptable in His sight.
For we are children of the light, greatly loved, a priesthood eternally blessed.
Help us rely on Your strength and may we be filled in Your rest.
For You are not a fallen man, but God, eternally faithful, not one to lie.
You have promised us a blessing, and You have blessed, let heaven hear our rejoicing cry.
Our number is great by thy mercy, our might is formed where we were weak.
Lead us to Your Holy purpose, Lead our people with the humble and meek.
For apart from You, we are sheep of great number without a shepherd; we are lost in the desert, we are a people most wretched and blemished as a leper.
Put us through the purifying fire, the fire of Holiness, the fire of war.
Let us lean not on our own understanding,
don't let us trust man anymore.
For you are our God, we are Your people submitted to Your corrective rod.
As a loving Father You chastise us, we have matured as a great tree grown from fertile sod.
Let the rivers in our life, no longer be called Mara or bitter.

Let them flow with Your life, bringing health to our
roots, give us truth to consider.
Lead us to the promised land, For we know in faith
who You are.
Multiply us in humility, may we see Your prophecy
unfold as our number is countless as the stars.
For You are God alone, the one who has delivered us
from the world.
Grace has been our victory, and we wave strong in
the wind as an adorned banner unfurled.
Number our people, for we do not number
ourselves, let us be one under Your name.
For our number is made great by Your presence,
no matter what we may attain.
All the glory to You, may our number be a
testimony of Your eternal Love.
May our people be known by You alone
in the book of life written above.

Remember Me

Remember me, oh believer, remember me I cry.
For when I am forgotten in your generation
it is then destined to suffer and die.
I am the ever flowing river, the true vine,
the brazen serpent of salvation.
Turn not away from me, for I am a jealous God, and
desire you to be a sanctified and holy nation.
Remember me in your affairs, your details, and all
your going.
For in remembrance of me the blessing of grace will
be freely flowing.
Remember my law written inside of your heart.
Be consecrated fully to me and unto the world leave
no part.
Remember to abandon the great cities that my
power has overcome.
For holding but a token of it will devour your soul
beyond sum.
Give unto me the whole of your heart; leave no room
for sin's occasion.
Remember my warnings of love, remember I am with
you in advance and invasion.
Remember me child, for there is still much more of
me to learn.
Keep me close and I will draw closer, I will answer
when you cry and yearn.
Remember me and my glory that I revealed to you in
measure.

Remember that I love thee greatly and you were created for my good pleasure.
Tell all your friends, strangers, and generations to proceed.
That you have the Almighty God at thy side and on My word all can grow and feed.
Remember me and my purpose for you and others, my Holy priest.
Remember I gave great promise when you were among the least.
Remember me child for as you conquer evil
I am prone to be forgot.
I know you will leave me in your exaltation, but leaving you I will not.
I am forever faithful, with you, for you, loving you all through your life.
I am forgotten and left behind, but in grace I will remove sin's knife.
Yes that was you accusing me and nailing me to that cross.
Yes I am forgotten, but I have come into your world to save that what was lost.
No matter the offense, it stands eternally forgiven at that tree.
You are my pearl of precious price; I will be there when you cry remember me.

Oceans of Apathy: A Cry for the Fisherman of Light

Order my steps before you let them be directed.
Keep my prayers before thee and my heart Father,
perfect it.
In the darkest depth of my life your rod it comforts
me.
For your line of grace and hook of love saves me
from the death in this sea.
Out of drowning in the ocean of shame and despair,
My spots, my depravity from the darkness, I cannot
stomach, leave me in the depths that's my prayer.
No you cry as you pull me into the depths of light.
Your spots are precious to me; you are beautiful in
my sight.
I break the surface into the open air, it is then I see a
man.
Bruised, broken, almost grotesque and
He is holding out his hand.
He then speaks and says by my wounds you are
justified by my bruises you are made free.
It is then the fisherman is transfigured right before
me.
The light so great, the glory words cannot explain.
But now I know this fisherman has not caught me up
in vain.
Because in this display of glorious and divine light.
My spots reflect spectrums of color my depravity is
turned to might.

In this display of strength, and glory oh how I long to have stayed there.
But a wave has come upon me and
the current has become my snare.
I am once again in the ocean, in its darkest depths and plans.
In desperation I grab all the hooks
in hope I will meet that man.
Left and right I am lost my moment
of rapture it has passed me by.
It is then I hear it a still small voice and a distinct cry.
Qualified, finished, for you that display was done.
So that this ocean will be lit by my glory and
you hold onto your salvation.
I in my doubt and fear this voice is a lie.
For in this darkness the hooks are not made in love
but made so that I will die.
Destruction surely is my path I cannot avoid these hooks as I can't see them.
The voice then cries let your light shine,
let it lead you back to Him.
If this is you, I have no light apart from what you presented.
The voice then declares that was the past my light is eternally cemented.
In the facets of your spots in the deepness of your depraved soul;
My light is made perfect as it is my secret place that you may be made whole.
Oh what a truth my sickness and shame is vanquished forevermore.

No, this is not darkness around me this is the place I was made for.
Let your light so shine before all men.
For in our oceans of apathy more are lost in their sin.
In the eternal darkness, if they continue to be left alone, trapped and grabbed by every hook of hate without a soul caring or hearing their moan.
But I say unto you my light was not imputed
in your life in vain.
Let the world hear of the lines of grace and
the fisherman that was slain.
But remember as you saw that fisherman was made new.
It is this message, this truth, to the sea I send you.
Those waves were not foreseen, at least by your eyes.
But by mine I allowed it so my imparted light could be realized.
For my truth is sharp and pierces into the deepest depths of your soul.
Be comforted by my imparted light, and in my truth of life be abundant and full.
For in this life all can made whole, in My light all can be made whole.

I am For You: My First Love Forgotten

I find myself in deep despair I have left my first love
and run to destruction.
Sleeping with death I find no care or wisdom,
there is no hope or instruction.
Sowing the wind, the whirlwind must come
my end is drawing nigh.
A life selling my heart to the highest bid my enemies
have encompassed me to buy.
given everything I ever needed, filled in all things and
exalted by my first love; I have left a great blessing
and fly alone as a misguided dove.
Away from my home, my nest from which my
first love carefully provided; I have severed all ties, I
am sold to many masters my soul is broken and
divided.
I abide in a city where my riches and fame are ever
growing and multiplied.
Although high and mighty among many lovers,
I find myself ever emptier inside.
Left in this life of many affairs, I see a great lion
observing my way.
Though it could devour me it circles about showing
mercy every day.
As if it has a love, a love that I once knew.
Giving me grace amidst my weakness where no
mercy is due.
Such great power of love that keeps its claws
contained.

It chastens my heart heavily and I perceive it as a warning that its wrath may not be forever retained.
Sold to highest bidders again and again, I find myself depreciated and of no value anymore.
There is then this cloaked stranger who seeks me out buying me with the highest score.
Bought for fifteen pieces of the finest silver, and for an homer of barley at the highest price.
I am of no value I cry and I am jaded by shame for committing the greatest of vice.
Unveiling himself, I melt within as I come to realize.
It is my first love, the lion that observed my ways yet still beholding me as beauty before His eyes.
Unfaithful I have been, and unfaithful I fear I will continue to be.
My first love responds no matter how much I am forgotten forever faithful will I be to thee.
I will continue to extend my merciful hand even when you sleep in affair with death.
For it is life I want to invest in you, my love is given unto my dying breathe.
I will be as the morning dew unto you, and as a lily you shall flourish and grow.
Your roots will run deep in my love and your beauty will branch out for all to know.
That your first love will love forever, loving you even when you unfaithfully stray.
Although you deserve great destruction, my grace is offered as my anger is turned away.

For in my grace to you, fruit will be found my love
will abound and your newly bestowed beauty will
eclipse all shame that you once knew.
You will look upon your branches as a green fir tree
and know that I graciously love and restore the
adulteress ones like you.
Although you are battered by those you sold yourself
so cheap, so shallow is no matter to be considered
anymore.
For your first love is for you always, even when evil is
within your heart's door.
Faithful to the unfaithful it is my character to love
the broken unconditionally without exception.
I hear your heart's yearning, but I will never see your
imperfection.
As far as the east is from the west so far have I
removed thy adulteress transgressions from thee.
I am forever at your side offering intercession so that
I may impart the greatest of beauty.
Sleeping with death will no longer render us apart.
For you are mine my love, I am for you, always
faithful, your name is eternally written upon my
heart.

The Righteous Restore

There is a generation that no longer knows Your
name.
Your servant has been forgotten and they seek their
own riches and fame.
Turning from Your covenant signed in unfailing love.
We choose graven idols and do evil in Your sight
from above.
We do not know our state, a righteous one must
come to restore.
To show this lost generation our idols will fail us
and You are much more.
For You are the righteous God that created us
all to bear Your appearance.
Instead of using our lives for worship we have
given the enemy free course and clearance.
We will be overcome by the snare laid out by their
false gods.
We will fall to slavery and be subject to our enemy's
oppressive rods.
You know this and have given us a way that will
overcome.
But even with warning, we run to the evil and live in
their ways as we are rendered spiritually blind and
dumb.
No longer able to see Your face, no longer able
to hear Your speech.
We need the righteous to restore us and
lead us out of the enemy's reach.

We are in no need of a ruler as we do what is right in our own eyes.

What we need is a righteous judge to adjust our way to Your way and dismiss the many lies.

To overcome our enemy and lead us to a victory with lasting peace; we cannot live in this circumstance anymore as our troubles only increase.

We praise You Lord for the righteous judge; he has restored us to walk in Your way.

We have a peace and a rest; it is here we will surely stay.

But there is a generation that no longer knows Your holy name.

Your righteous servant has been forgotten and they seek their own riches and fame.

Reverting back to what is right in their own eyes.

Ignorant that their ways are once again leading to destruction and their demise.

We fall so easily to our lust and our greed; we serve the king of Moab and worship his idol mammon.

Rich and famous we will become, but in this life there will be poverty and famine.

As we are quenching Your spirit and drained of all its conviction and care.

"they shall be as thorns in your sides and their gods shall be unto you a snare".

Your word is truth why do we error and forsake Your path?

Lord spare us from this enemy, send the righteous to restore us out from Your wrath.

You have placed us among our enemy as we have forgotten our way to war.
We lie subject to others and their opinions, but only Your truth can restore.
Touching what is unclean the corruption has followed.
We have chosen a way against Thee and the deceit of it is what we have swallowed.
Destroying us from within, we cannot find a way to avoid its fee.
The righteous restore us, lead us back to You and set us free.

I will deliver you in covenant love, my mercy I will pour out.
I will raise up a valiant warrior that will defeat your enemy with a small company and a shout.
You will leave me again, I will allow you to stray.
For no matter how many times you seek a path you will find I am the only way.
I will not deliver you for a time, as there is a price for your choice.
You will live in consequence, but I will be by your side when you choose to hear my voice.
You will find better circumstance is not your savior, salvation is who I am.
A righteous judge may restore peace, but there is no peace apart from the Lamb.
For the Lamb is set on the altar to restore the depths within your darkened heart.

It is here that the war is won and here that the enemy can be stopped before it starts.
Build unto me an altar, I will provide the sacrificial Lamb.
It is my heart's desire for you to live free from sin's grasp and grow to know who I am.
I created you to be a holy nation, a wife, a bride to be present at my throne.
To reign with me forever and eternally be glorified as you will be known.
By the most High God, The king of kings and Lord of Lords, Eternally secure in an Identity of Christ, singing in endless song playing endless chords.
This is my plan for you, you are glorious in my sight.
Turn no more to the lies before you and seek me in the night.
There is no judge like me, for none can eternally settle the case.
There is none righteous and none have the power over sin to appease and erase.
There are none upon a cross apart from my Son.
Who in death found victory and in death your souls were won.
The Righteous restore, but among the righteous there is only one.
Who can take a wretch like me and call me a holy priest and a son.
The Righteous restore as I will only run away.
But the Lord draws me close into a relationship that nothing can hinder or sway.

The Righteous restore even when I ally with deception.
What love is this that sees no sin and holds for me an open reception?
The Righteous restore may the imperfect judges remind me every day; that my circumstance is not my problem it is my heart and my soul's way.
The Righteous restore even when there is no king within my life.
Doing what is right in my own eyes; The Lord will lend His sight and save me from my strife.
The Righteous restore there is no other way, no higher decree.
The Righteous God above will exalt those washed by the living water pouring out from the Cross at Calvary.
?

Seekers Cry: God's Reply

I feel I have been forgotten, by the Lord most high.
I pray fervently to Him, but his answers are not nigh.
I am burdened by my trials and drenched in my storms.
Where is my Savior in these times?
My doubt swells and fear forms.
I have been left out, downtrodden and destroyed.
I feel as if you left Lord, your promises are void.
I find in this feeling, there is none of You at all.
This is my guilt speaking and my doubts leading me to fall.
Your love has become my burden Your grace has become my shame.
All the good things You impart to me, I turn around and mock Your name.
This is Self-condemnation, for in it no good will live.
My guilt will poison any sweetness and my self-righteousness will nullify what You give.
I am not forgotten, but You Lord have I disremembered, I have lost sight of where we started.
I have hid within the garden with fig leaves as You call out with your grace imparted.
Ready to clothe me in Your provision hand-picked and slaughtered for me.
It is not just coats of skin, it is a perfect Lamb that You gave to set me free.
I did not ask for more, although I chose the knowledge of sin.

It is You I must not forget, and a rest I must find in Your provision.

Knowledge of good and evil, but good is all I should have known.

In sight of your goodness Lord, I can eat of the tree of life and be in your presence at the throne.

One more thing, as if I had lacked before.

I was created in Your image, given eternal provision and life forevermore.

I was not created to judge, for in judgment I find myself tainted.

I cannot bear the illustration of what my sin has painted.

You are not Forgotten, this I hear you say.

Rise up again from your pit and follow my way.

Be transformed in my light; carry it into your darkest places.

For the light overcomes the darkness and will the fill the largest of spaces.

I call you to the water where you perceive you will sink.

But it is here I liberate your spirit and truly empower you to think.

To see that you have depth, and capacity beyond compare; For in my presence, you are free to try new things and openly share.

You will find no restrictions, as the deep has no end.

If you fail, I lift you up and if you stray into the dark blind, unto you a light I send.

As the depths are endless, it is so with my grace.

For no sin I see, I have removed it when my Son took its place.

For I only can see you in a Father's love, and in deep compassion.

For you are my sons and daughters, crucified in many fashions.

I no longer see the sin spare its suffering and pain it puts on you.

In love I send you comfort and a living word that resonates true.

May the words resonate in your soul and lead to deeper relation with who I am.

I am so much more than a God of judgment demanding sacrifice of the lamb.

I am God that loves, even in your hate.

I am God that forgives and a God that can relate.

I am God that knows all and in everything I persist.

I am God that hears your prayers and God that will assist.

I am God that see's your pain and sends comfort in its place.

I am God that keeps my covenant to you, your offense towards me is erased.

I am God that imparts righteousness, when evil persists and abides.

I am God that is with you and forever at your side.

You are not forgotten, perceive your sin no more.

Your offenses are cleared, I have settled the score.

I am not Forgotten, I am forever in Your sight.

Though I run away in guilt and I hide in the darkness of night.
You are always there knowing all that I am in.
You know everything about me, but choose not to see my sin.
The one worthy to judge me, I find grace in Your courts offered to me unrestricted.
Lord preserve my way in your presence for in my self-condemnation great burdens are inflicted.
Not by works of righteousness I have done, but by what I have been given.
Lord this life, this provision must I rest and your mercy be what I live in.
I see through a glass darkly, but through You all is made clear.
Save me from my condemnation and rescue me from my fear.
Cover me in Your grace oh God for in it I must rest.
I am not anything apart from You just a lost bird from its nest.
May I be comforted by Your words, for in them I find my might.
I am victoriously chosen for the good fight.
I am not forgotten I am forever in Your sight.

Finding Grace

Why have I found grace in thine eyes,
When I am from a past and a people despised?
Why have I found grace in thy sight, when I come
from a line of bitterness and a sore plight?
Having no name, no people spare my mother in law.
Working among Your people it is virtue You saw.
Why have I found grace in thine eyes, I am an
outcast, a daughter of the idolaters of the
uncircumcised?
Adopting a life, a God I have yet to know.
You offer me a dwelling and a part in a
blessing that will forever flow.
Let my people be your people and Thy God be thy
God.
Let death part thee and me for apart from You I am
dust and sod.
Devoted I will be to thee, in Your law and provision
will I live.
For out in this world apart from thee there is
not a portion I would have, and not a part of me
would I give.
For in your heritage, in this nation of holy priest; I am
counted as a part of the fold when I was among the
least.
Against you, my nature, my lineage will always be.
But I found grace and a Love from above that has set
me free.

Redeemed to a people when I was apart from its mold, I am redeemed to be part of a story that forever will be told.

For He that has begun a work will complete it until the end.

I, a stranger have been counted a blessing and a close friend.

In a time, in a period where all the men do what is right in their own eyes.

You choose to dwell with me and be there steadfast in my helpless cries.

From an empty bitter house to a family that considers one such as You.

I am counted among the saints, the faithful, the remnant of few.

Just as I was accepted, the One that follows accepts all; considering the publicans and sinners, the diseased and the least among the fall.

I am finding grace in places that bear burdens of hurt and bitter pain.

I am finding grace in the house of outcast separated from You oh Lord by Sin's stain.

Why have I found grace in thine eyes, when in my heart I have spat on the beloved Son as He dies?

As He died, CRUCIFY is what I shouted within my fallen soul.

As the weight of my sin was carried by each drop of His blood that now makes me whole.

I have found grace in Thine sight, an exile far outside.

No matter how far the distance, Your outstretching arm accepts all and faithfully provides.

I, like the one before, so long ago; is now redeemed to be part of a Holy nation, set apart for the Almighty God to love and know.

Working among the fields no more than a laborer of little renown; I am now set before You with Your Son and bearing a crown.

A crown of righteousness, though within myself I find none, A crown that I cast before Your feet as it was You that redeemed me and through You my life was hidden in the Son.

A victorious life, despite my denial and disaster; finding grace, what a treasure as I serve a great and faithful Master.

A master that offers protection and deals mercifully and just;

A master that has set me aside, paid the price for my heart, and a master waiting for me as a faithful bridegroom that I can trust.

To take me as His own, when I was before the cross an adversary to be condemned. . .

Finding Grace from the Lord Jesus that took my sin to the tomb where it is forever forgotten in Him. . .

Just as the mother sought redemption for her estranged daughter

I, greatly loved by You have found grace as You are my living bread and water.

For away from You I began, close will I be in the end. As Your body was broken for me, my deep wounds of sin did You tend.

Finding grace, let it be what I forever pursue.

For there is none to be found in this world apart
from You.
Finding grace, let it be what illuminates my life.
For in His stripes I was healed and in finding grace He
has taken me as a precious wife.
⁇

Caught in His Grace

So caught up in Your Grace God I can feel it.
When I read in your pages I'm saved and you spirit
has sealed it.
Lord keep me near it, don't let me fear it.
Keep me walking in the faith that allows me to hear
it.
It is Your grace that wakes me in the morning and
evening.
It is Your grace that keeps me breathing.
Oh to look upon my sin with mercy.
The thought of how you do that daily hurts me.
The filth the wrath, all that I have done wrong.
You tell me in your word it is finished I have new
song.
Lord can it be that I'm completely forgiven.
Even when my lies, lust, and pride stays persistent.
I want to know how to live a life full of Your grace.
If not full of it Lord, please just give me a taste.
Just like a great meal cooking down the hall.
The smell brings joy and I feel a call.
But instead of carnal food and a carnal table,
I find myself at Your feet secure and stable.
Keep me caught up in Your grace as my flesh
restrains, The grace that is stored in heaven
for me proclaiming Jesus reigns.
Oh Lord how I could write of your grace in endless
psalms.
Keep me at your throne head down with uplifted
palms.

So caught up in your grace I don't want to leave.
But Your spirit is ringing and I have a call to receive.
I hear it in Your word Go and tell the
world of this scandalous grace.
Don't let a soul turn away, don't neglect one face.
I see this set before me and I feel ashamed
and unfit to do it all.
Thank you God it is finished I will answer the call.

Transformed to His way

The word is all I need, The life of Christ is
what I cling to and hold.
It is this profound word of grace that empowers me
to speak of truth and be bold.
Somehow I have affected lives and turned
them to look towards you.
When I feel so distant and selfish in all that I do,
I have affected a life with Your work in me, this I
cannot explain.
A life has been directed to seek You Lord and rely on
Your grace to sustain.
I pray for this life, for they may not always be on
Your path.
For it is not me that saved them, but You that spared
them from the Father's wrath.
Don't let us condemn ourselves as we are constantly
caught in sin's snare.
Teach us your grace pouring out, instruct us in Your
word leave nothing to spare.
Give us a great hunger for Your truth it is the only
thing that gives us vitality.
Pull us away from our many circumstances and
put us into the true reality.
The reality of Your presence forever at our side.
The reality that it is in our hearts that You forever
abide.
The reality that You love us all and deeply care.
The reality that All is finished and we can rest as
Christ has paid our fare.

The reality that You desire to do a mighty work within.

The reality that we are no longer defined by what we have done or our current sin.

The reality that You provide in our many situations.

The reality that You transcend our doubt and use us to reach the nations.

The reality that we are valued at the highest price covered by Your blood.

The reality that Your grace is an ocean overflowing in our life raging as a flood.

The reality that we cannot ever hope to attain, but instead will choose to dwell in and rest.

The reality that You try us in trials and put our lives to the test.

The reality that through each trial we may come out as gold.

The reality that we can stand unbroken in brokenness when our calamity unfolds.

The reality that we are eternally known and seated at Your table.

The reality that Your word is our support always keeping us stable.

As our lives go separate ways, I pray You direct us where You will.

May we live in seeking You and Your portion from the Holy spirit be our fill.

Lord there is a truth that as I, through you, have affected one, now two can affect four.

For in You God there is power to share words of life and affect more.

Lord I pray for the life that has been affected by Your way in me.
May the life they saw be emanating in theirs also for all to see.
Bless their way and nourish all friendships that arise.
Rebuke the evil against them now and lift the veil from their eyes.
May they see you more as I am seeing You more each day.
Continue Your work in us oh God and may we be transformed to Your way.

⁇

Enlarge my heart

Lord Enlarge my heart till it is bursting at the seams.
Help me care for others, be the initiator of my faith
dreams.
Don't let me be wrapped up in the cares and
snares of this life.
Lift your banner of freedom high triumphant
over all pain and strife.
Stretch me, teach me, be everything, beseech me.
The hard questions, the long answers, the endless
songs,
Keep enlarging my heart, keep me growing strong.
Help me be a student a hearer of your word.
Help me not just receive but given to those who
haven't heard.
Enlarge my heart keep me in your presence forever.
Singing songs and praises, Lord this relationship none
can sever.
Me at your feet, You on your throne.
Imparting righteousness to me and my sins atoned.
Enlarge my heart to the extent to where I trust.
That your Word is sharper and your grace is just.
Lord enlarge my heart for those out of reach.
Send your body out and your grace and truth be
what they teach.
Lord I'm a leech, to You I cling.
Enlarge my heart to where it is solely Your song that I
sing.
Enlarge my heart for it is You I love.

Because of this, the lost world is what I'm thinking
of.
The Middle East where they are so mislead by fear.
Lord, these people I pray your love to be
acknowledged and all they hear.
Asia, their minds being emptied for a
Knowledge they will never know.
Lord enlarge my heart so your truth
and wisdom is what I show.
Europe, Africa, those that remain.
Enlarge my heart Lord with a love that will sustain.
As they put grace away as a picture of the past,
Oh it's Your grace and heart that will outlast.
Enlarge my heart it is an endless plea,
because out my heart no love will flow naturally.
Enlarge my heart it is a helpless plea.
For out of my heart is spite and degeneracy.
Enlarge my heart Lord it is what I cherish.
For I know without Your heart this whole world
would have perished.

. . .

Call me to Another

Call me to another for the one that you send me
to is wretched and unclean.
Call me to another for what business do I have with
the heathen, the wicked and the mean.
Call me to another the bitterness I have towards the
ones you send me is greater than their despair.
Call me to another leave that city to its coming
doom let the people pay the fare.
I have no place among a nation, you do not call your
own.
These people you have sent me to
have no place among your throne.
I will proclaim your message, these
people surely will not accept.
They are a people full of wickedness and greatly
inept.
Still you keep me on course, to the place I dare not
go.
Lord hear me this last time, these people will
not receive they will not grow.
Cut them off from the earth, cut them off from my
sight.
You send me there to judge them, now judge
them now for their plight.
Depart I will, this call is not for me.
Call me to another, these people cannot go free.
Forever in my sight, you run but you cannot
flee from my commands.
Go unto the distant city, I will turn you

over to the heathen's hands.
Through your defiance, my name will still be
glorified.
The heathen among you on the ship will proclaim my
name as they are horrified.
I called you to minister; I have included your
account in my holy word.
To show that I am God, even among the unwilling
prophet where my commands go unheard.
I will perform a work in you until the
day of the Lord has come.
In the belly of the whale three days, I will
use you as a sign for my Son.
For greater is the purpose of the God who formed
your heart.
Greater is His purpose no matter how great thou art.
For among the unwilling prophet, many will be set
free.
His sign, a type, one that will be known eternally.
For greater is the Man, my Son resurrected from the
tomb.
Greater is the one that comes to save those that you
refuse to love and leave to their doom.
How great is the need to go into the places
we say call me to another.
When among the very people we despise, God has
called
out a sister and a brother.
Let Jonah not be your mold in which you mold your
heart.

For a heart filled with bitterness will harden and ruin you before you start.
Call me to another let this be our cry for more.
As we reach out to all the nations and go out with what God created us for.
Call me to another for the hearts here all have received.
Call me to another that is broken and deceived.
Call me to another don't let another perish while I am on this earth.
Call me to another, to share of Your grace, your story, Your Holy Son's spiritual birth.
Let not the deception of this world cloud our eyes with hate.
For those that have done wrong or those who are proclaimed second rate.
Call me to another one that is delving into despair.
One that is waiting for redemption in a world filled with destruction and no care.
Call me to another, although their offenses may be great.
For there is none that You desire to perish and there is none forsaken in Sin's fate . . . Call me to Another

Refuge in Thy Wandering

Lost in the fields I cannot find my way,
a lion stalks in the darkness seeking whom he will
slay.
A shepherd diligently seeking the lost sheep that is I,
but the darkness is thick with fog the shepherd
cannot find me, I surely am destined to die.
The air weighs heavy on my back
I am paralyzed by a roaring lie.
The roar so great, so confident, I will never return to
where I belong as I cannot hear the shepherds cry.
He cries out into the night diligently seeking by the
day.
But the lion has had my scent for a while now,
I am weak and easy prey.
My ears now rendered useless, my eyes
deceive me in the haze.
I will never see the green pastures or feel secure as
my shepherd is nowhere to be seen in this maze.
Wandering since birth, I was lost since I came into
this being.
The lion had snatched me from the fold and I am
forever in his preying game, blind unseeing.
The time has come, I feel the claws,
I am ensnared in this fate I was made for the lion's
jaws.
Oh, but only to wound, I am a game for the lion's
scheme.
Now wounded lying in my dirty blood,
I am infected now death is my theme.

Is there even a shepherd, a man that cares?
For I have been in this lion's game for ages and
constantly caught in his snares.
I am useless, deformed, evil in my thinking and
diseased.
I hope for the lion to end this despair and
the law in this land will be appeased.
Then I feel it, a hand reach down from what I can
only perceive as light.
Out of my bloody pit, a Savior has come with love
and has deferred the lion's plight.
He speaks with words I have never heard before.
I have been searching for you wandering one, you
are broken but I sought you to restore.
I will restore your ears first so you may tune out the
lions roaring threats.
For it is my words you will now hear and I will
remove those years of damage and regrets.
This can't be true, I say, as I am disfigured by the
lion's endless lies.
The voice ignores my doubt and then restores my
eyes.
Then I see Him, not a shepherd but an anointed king.
With a crown of thorns and hands pierced by nails I
feel responsible as in His search for me he met this
suffering.
As if He knew my thoughts, he responds it was worth
it all, The lion cannot hope to prevail.
For that lion is just a defeated foe,
it is finished I have broken the fogs looming veil.

You now have your legs, and are so precious in my sight.
Go forth find more sheep wounded in the night.
I, in fear cannot, as I remember the claws and the terrible bite.
I have given you strength, The Lord responds, rest in my peace and fight.
You are as white as snow, you will always reflect my glory.
you will see the lion and stand strong for he no longer has a hold on your story.
Hear my voice, the roar will be nothing compared to my word;
for it is my name that will be known eternally and to others through you it will be heard.
I respond in courage, Not only to hear but to step, not only to step but in faith to leap.
Lord it is your word that I will keep.
Into the darkness I find a truth that I never knew was there.
The lion is actually an evil man leading sheep astray into thorns and tares.
The Lord is my shepherd, I shall not want he leadeth me beside still waters.
but in my blindness and deafness of sin the lion enslaved me in endless struggle and slaughter.
Even now I am constantly trapped even with the Lord's imparted light.
For even when I have been restored I refuse to hear the Lord's voice and keep him in sight.

Oh to hear the word of God, for the Lord is truly
divine.
He found me in a pit bearing the a cross saying you
are mine.
Oh what a love, to take the nails
and carry a cross for my shame.
For without it I couldn't have been reached
in the pit where I laid lame.
Now white as snow my crimson has been wiped
away.
In the Lord's speaking distance, near
the heavenly house will I stay.
He leads me out to pastures full of sheep in despair.
With a message of hope, with legs, eyes and
obedient ears I speak and share.
of the Father's love, His unending grace
A description of his majesty, of his
sacrifice so all may see His face.
The Lord is thy refuge in thy wandering a
very present help in time of trouble.
Therefore we will not fear though the earth be
removed and our soul, in sin, is reduced to rubble.
Though the lions roar, though the mountains shake
and swell,
I tell those in their pits, you are free, liberated,
and justified although you fell.
Hear the Lord's voice crying, be still and know that I
am God.
I will be exalted among all and on my sheep the lion
will not prevail or defraud.
Refuge in thy wandering, The Lord will always be.

For in His great love he sought my soul, died, overcame death and set me free.

☐

Rest in Me

Rest in me for there is no other way.
Rest in me for I have given you this day.
Rest in me for I have the words of Life.
Rest in me as I have freed you from your sin and strife.
Rest in me as I see your affliction,
Rest in me for in my righteousness I give benediction.
Rest in me as my flesh has been torn with hands and feet nailed to a cross.
Rest in me for in my sacrifice you do not have to pay that cost.
Rest in me as my word will impart infinite light.
Rest in me and be counted precious in my sight.
Rest in me as there are no others to rest in in this world.
Rest in me for from my voices
utterance this universe unfurled.
Rest in me as I know you better than
anyone you have ever known.
Rest in me for I am above all and in all longing for your presence at my throne.
Rest in me as it is finished the war is fought and won.
Rest in me for I have sent on your account a blameless one.
Rest in me as I know that your flesh is evil in its decay.
Rest in me for I have a new life in which you can live free and eternally stay.
Rest in me as my provision will never be outdone.

Rest in me for I Am that I Am in need of nothing, and
sent you my only Son.
Rest in me as I have drawn you from the depths of
death and have brought you to the surface.
Rest in me for you are now adopted sons and
daughters, saints with an eternal purpose.
Rest in me as I am the only way.
Rest in Me for My eternal presence will not ever go
away.
The cry rings out, it takes root in my troubled soul.
But its truth is far from my mind
and its simplicity is not effectual.
Oh Lord give me rest, for my soul is
ever troubled, restless on its own.
Remind me of Your grace and your gift of
life in which all my sin was atoned.
Oh Lord give me rest, for I cannot
find comfort and any verity.
Remind me of your lovingkindess,
your Hesed and your loving Charity.
Oh Lord give me rest, for my soul longeth after thee.
Remind me that you hear my prayers and
do not leave me in my helpless plea.
Oh Lord give me rest, for my circumstance
has become my king.
Remind me of your joy, your songs and
The peace amidst my suffering.
Oh Lord give me rest, for my affliction has
Certainly gained its ground.
Remind of your promises, the surety of them, your
faithfulness to draw me at the trumpets sound.

I recall in my mind, that I have an eternal hope in thee.
Your compassions fail not and your
new mercies cry "Rest in Me".

Psalms 86:10
"For thou art great, and doest wondrous things:
thou art God alone."

My Worship
Great God Almighty, how great are thy works.
They testify of your power and root out all evil where
it lurks.
Great God Almighty, wondrous are your ways.
Your light goes before me you lead me all my days.
Great God almighty your wisdom none
can fathom with the mind.
For your knowledge leads us towards love and
your wisdom of grace is kind.
Great God almighty you are God alone.
A new heart you have given, a heart of
flesh for my heart of stone.
Great God Almighty, words fall short of exclaiming
an endless soliloquy of your beauty and a love
that is never waning.
Great God Almighty teaching me, instructing me,
keeping me on a perfect path.
Though I may stumble and fall, your outflowing
mercy and
grace is the aftermath.
Great God Almighty above all that may exalt itself on
high.
Great God Almighty to you will I draw nigh.

My Wonder

May I never lose the wonder,
the wonder of your way.
It keeps my heart inclined to worship, it
restrains my sinful stray.
May I only worship You, in your presence may I sing:
Of the knowledge of your resurrection power and
fellowship with your suffering.
May I diligently seek you, for my life is ever on
display.
Keep those who observe me from failing of your
grace.
To think my ways are watched, Lord please don't let
anyone be deceived.
The good they see me doing is only
out of what I have received.
Faith is what I need as I take a step off the edge.
Towards those whom I love and
to You whom my life is pledged.
Help me lay down my life before your throne as I go
explore.
The wonderful world you have created and enter
into other's lives that you adore.
Just a perspective, a glimpse of what you see on
high,
For my faith is weak, and my message is distorted to
a lie.
Purify my lips as I dwell in the land of the unclean.
To your word and imparted purity, Lord to this I
cling.

My Life

Lord my life is bought; to you my life is laid.
For your Son exclaimed "it is Finished"
forever my price is paid.
May I live worthy of your calling as
I am just an earthen vessel of flesh and bone.
May your breath of life sweep into my dry valley and
change my heart of stone.
The stone, it was rolled away to reveal your empty
tomb.
But lord now my life is dead and
I need a new life to be exhumed.
To live is Christ and to die is gain
let this be my life's lasting cry.
As I weep over the friends and
family who have been deceived by Satan's lie.
On my knees Lord, let this be where my battles are
led.
And your living word, burning in my bones, by this
I'm fed.
Let me know no man by the flesh, for we all fail,
and fall short of expectation.
Lord in my judgmental state will I destroy and
throw others into damnation.
Don't let this be! for their hearts I truly care.
May your love dwell richly in my life
and grace be what I share.
Great Almighty God, Lord of Lords and King of Kings.
My worship, my wonder, and my life
to You I devote these things.

I Dare You

I dare you to take a step closer, closer to the reality
that is Me.
I dare you to look around and go to places
you thought were out of reach.
I dare you to pursue me with all your strength and
might.
I dare you because your life is guided by my Light.
I dare you to walk into the dark ministering my
verity.
I dare you to be bold and confident; In Me is your
Identity.
I dare you because no one else would dare.
To take you out of the mundane life and into My
care.
I dare you because in Me you are truly free.
To become and prosper as who you were always
meant to be.

Much of the least of things

You make much of the least of things, a concept I
cannot comprehend or bear.
You make much of great suffering,
I know you were not
its author but why must I continue.
Much of the least of things, you have made a
mansion out of a condemned venue.
Why must I endure in such great pain, what is there
to advance my cause when all I feel is the rain?
Great I thought I was, but tribulation has been the
norm.
Why must I be surrounded in silence in prosperity
and great counsel and wisdom in the storms?
Your ways are not my ways; Your thoughts are
nowhere near what I have thought.
Much of the least of things, why have I not
attained what I desperately sought?
A broken vessel full of hope, leaking from
the cracks and blemishes throughout.
A field of great fruit, filled with water,
but constantly in drought.
Much of the least of things, why must You operate
this way?
Why must my ability be made of no value, and
my weakness be what You value and cherish?
I am beginning to realize it is the least of things
within that allow me to grow where others may
perish.

For much of the least of things, is the cry of humanity
as we will look unto Your great throne.
Redeemed, made new, given life in grace and
nothing less.
You make much of the least of things, beauty out our
mess.
What strength is there within weakness, and
what greatness is there among the meek?
What boldness is there among the timid, and
what courage is among the weak?
You have made much of the least of things,
the least of things being me.
I am here: low self-esteem, insecure, unsure,
and unwilling to move on.
You have made much of me and have given me a
new song.
Why is it we find rest in the things
that imminently are our destruction?
Why is it that our ears will close when
we are given a revelation of You and healthy
instruction?
Much of the least of things no matter our flaws or
imperfections,
You have advanced the weakest over the strong,
contrary to our finest collections.
How can the ideas from our minds transcend a
mind that is eternal, and far above?
Much of the least of things, believe this and
you too will experience a great love.
No matter the questions, the doubts, the guilt, the
shame and the fear found within.

No matter the reason the intellect or IQ we may
achieve.
God has set His way so all can come unto Him and
receive.
A life everlasting, a life that my
words could not begin to explain,
Volumes of grace, a endless revelation and
a truth that no books can contain.
We look to a book, the Bible, just a fraction of
revelation in our darkened eyes. Its author is
eternally existent and full of great character and
love.
For much of the least of things God has made
all things so that we may look to Him above.
So no matter what gaps or questions unanswered
within what we can perceive from revelation given to
us here below.
There is a life behind truth that will give depth to the
smallest revelation, an eternal source that will
forever flow.
Much of the least of things, let my life
be a testament of its verity.
For in the once insecure, unsure, and stressed soul
there is now peace, joy, love and great clarity.
Much of the least of things, no
matter how great you may think you are.
For what greatness do you have when your life is but
a blip upon existence among the sun our morning
star?
You are but dust, the sooner you
realize this the better your life can be.

For in the revelation of being the least of things, there is a hope of being made much dwelling with God in eternity.

Rebuilding the Temple

I am the ruined temple one that stood glorious
before.
I am the broken vessel, a bag torn and tattered in
which nothing can be stored.
I am cursed and hopeless as I reap little of what I
have sown.
I stand unclean before You, tainted,
and unworthy before Your throne.
You commission me to build a new temple one that
will be. filled with glory greater than what once
stood,
One built with lesser material,
one of common stones and wood.
I stand before You bitter, not moved to perform this
task.
For what benefit is it to build of the least
and carry out what You ask?
Forsaken I truly am, left in ruin beyond repair.
For what profit is it to build lesser and
be seen as the weeds and tares.
How can a place be Holy, unless it be greatly
adorned?
How can I stand before others as nothing,
an object open to be scorned?
How will others know that I serve the Almighty God
When the temple you instruct me to build is
no greater than the rubble and sod?
How can we stand in power, or as a blessing to the
world?

When we stand as a remnant, outcast in
lands where foreign flags are unfurled?
How may we bring in Your kingdom
when we have not a king to reign?
We have nothing but a broken city being rebuilt in
vain.
Still I hear You call, from the messenger you have
sent.
I am stirred by your faithfulness
and by his persistence I am bent.
Consider your ways, this is what the Lord of host has
said.
You have dwelt to long in ruin, in a covering
that will not cover the bed.
For in this meek and lowly temple,
there is greater glory to be shown
For within this temple God will eternally be
seated upon His throne.
A temple less adorned but covered in His love.
A temple with the greater glory of God from above.
For what can be said about the least among the
people?
What can be said of the remnant congregating
under a worn steeple?
For we know the greater glory
goes to the meekest of them all.
The one full of power, that upon the cross chose to
fall
A man born of a virgin, of a woman of
no fame or great descent.
A common man of Nazareth, a Galilean, a teacher,

a sacrifice to be lent.
For what can a man say, of what we now hold inside?
A dwelling, a new temple that
the Almighty God will forever abide.
For no matter what glory we attain,
or what fame we can accrue.
Nothing transcends the glory of the
most holy temple broken for you.
Broken on a cross, a common tree for criminals
and the defamed.
Broken by a spear spilling out the very blood by
which we are now covered and named.
I make all things New it is His promise as the
temple was restored after three days.
Surrender your all to Christ and in your
temple he will establish His ways.
For no matter how lowly or mundane we think we
stand.
We are the temple of greater glory the broken
temple redeemed by nailed scarred hands.
⁇

Redemption is coming

Redemption is coming from the LORD of Host with armies great in glory.
Redemption is coming as it is always the intent of The Holy God's great story.
Desolation and famine is what you have known.
But redemption is coming and great glory
will be seated on the throne.
Great Zion, New Jerusalem. The New kingdom is come.
Redemption is coming accept the
Savior and put away Sin's sum.
Turn ye even to me with all your heart.
Redemption is coming as it is the Love of
God that sacrificed all from the start.
With fasting with weeping and with
mourning come to me solely.
Come unto your God, who is merciful and Holy.
Rend your hearts and not your garments,
for I look upon what is within.
Polished and righteous you may feign, but I Am sees the sin.
Turn unto the LORD your God for he is gracious and merciful slow to anger and of great kindness.
Redemption is coming from the clouds
with light to heal all the blindness.
I speak of the latter; please know redemption is already done.
It came of a virgin, adorned in the common things, but inwardly was God's Son.

Do not be downtrodden by what the locust,
cankerworm and caterpillar has eaten.
For no matter the circumstance, God has been with
you and all your enemies have been beaten.
Redemption is coming, it is by faith and
belief that it can come over you today.
Redemption is within the Cross of sacrifice
that ended the reign of Satan's way.
"Go your way", what a lie, what an injustice,
what a scheme and deception from below.
When in going your own way, you have fallen into
destruction that only the wrath of God can flow.
Be no longer deceived; be no longer
desolate among your barren fields.
Give God your heart and unto His will as your way
yields.
A yielded heart, God will greatly bless.
Redemption is coming, give yourself wholly to Him
and proclaim it to the rest.
Locust and plague will by no means be in your land
to stay.
Redemption is coming out of Zion, let
the barren land give ear to His way.
For our land is our heart, the inner man, our living
spirit.
The locust of Sin and judgment come in destruction,
but redemption is offered to all who will hear it.
Barren will our spirit be if we leave it devoid of truth.
A great mystery of brokenness never to be solved
by detective or sleuth.
Hear the cry of Joel, a prophecy of old but

also for our coming age.
A promise of great redemption out of the barren lands;
as wars prevail and rage.
A coming desolation, one greater than we can comprehend.
A crisis so dire that no plan or resistance will quell it or cause it to rend.
The wrath of God is severe;
do not think unrighteousness has gone ignored.
Accept the provision of grace that God has sent as He loves all, even the outcast and the abhorred.
Your life is eternal; it is eternally bought at great price.
Live the life more abundant, free from the bondage of sin,
the life found in Christ.
For as the land of Israel was laid waste in time before.
There is a greater field within our
heart that is barren, broken and scored.
Hard the ground has become as the
frost of sin has delved deep.
Unable to grow the beautiful things of life,
unable to harvest and reap.
Many things of destruction have been
sown into the barren land.
Redemption is coming; do not dwell here long,
and reach out to God's hand.
For outstretched God's arm has always been and forever until the day of the Lord will it persist.

Cultivate the hardened land, break thy fallow ground
and open your heart to the one you constantly resist.
Redemption is coming, look for the sheep bearing
a message among the many wolves.
Bearing a message of grace and liberty,
a message of hope and joy, a message for the
broken, a message for the hurting and blind, a
message for you, and a message for me.
Redemption is coming, listen to the Lord our God
come unto Him and see.

Beloved: A Letter From God

This is written to you, as you are My beloved
eternally on My mind.
Amidst your corruption, a total affront to my nature,
in you there is not one spot I find.
you are the apple of my eye,
my finest workmanship and forever mine.
you work so hard for my love even when you are
promised a great love, the most divine.
I see your trouble, I see all your afflictions.
If you could just for a moment look towards me, you
would be free from guilt and your judgmental
convictions.
I Am that I Am eternally faithful at your side.
Although many times you believe I have forsaken
you, I dwell in your heart where I forever abide.
I knock at its door to save you out of your world,
your perception and your prison that the enemy has
created.
I sent the most perfect sacrifice of my Son, on the
cross my desire for your freedom was translated.
I Am. in need of none of your work,
your talents, or your earthly treasure.
I gave all those things to you freely so you may be
filled with My grace beyond measure.
Lord I read your word, a love letter addressed to me.
But you don't relate to my sin as I do,
I am shortsighted and hardly free.
I acknowledge Your love Lord,
but its depths I cannot hope to hold.

Lord consider me no more,I am unworthy of this
love, I have so many times forsaken it and my heart
is so easily sold.
I cannot hope to reach you oh God, although Your
truth says its settled and done.
Lord in my heart there is oceans of apathy
and rejection of Your Son.
I hear this letter and cannot help but question in
disbelief.
among this wave of doubt I am feeling called to this
love you speak of and beginning to hope again in my
grief.
I pray now, for this letter to be received for
it is needful that I may grow.
For in my capacity I am incapable
to understand it, be secure and know.
That the love towards me is divinely given and
accepted,
Lord it must be more than a choice, more than a gift,
eternally sealed and protected.
Oh Lord here I go again, my world it
is troubled plagued in my strife. . .
He answers, Your world means to much to you,
I am God let me reign in your life.
I hear your prayers I long and cherish
for your presence before My throne.
For you are my son, greatly beloved, bought with the
highest price adopted as family, not as a slave to
own.
If you only knew the depths of My grace, My
unfailing, unconditional love towards thee.

What miracles you would witness and what
marvelous works and Identity you would have in Me.
you are free, the price is paid, but you constantly
cling to old chains.
You are the object of My love, I see nothing apart
from My Holy blood flowing in your veins.
I have given you My all, My most precious,
from you I ask the same.
but the price has been reduced by My blood as it is
finished, accept my life more abundant
and give your life of sin and shame.
I am and will be here bearing forth My arm
to take your sin's abuse.
My provision is waiting. forever yearning for your
use.
There is so much in store for you. here in heaven and
on earth.
I have known you before your existence, before your
family tree, before your birth.
I perceive you in love and grace is all I continue to
pour.
For I am your God, I change not, I will love you
forever more.
For I am God, I change not, I love you forever more.

A Call None Will Chase

There is a call none will chase.
their hearts are longing for it, but there need they never face.
The need to call out to the caller, as their ability is insufficient.
It is this call that is not heard as their pride clouds their eyes giving them a sense of omniscience.
For it is they who think they know how to do the work laid out in Your word.
But the still small voice in their ministry, oh Lord it is rarely heard.
Call out louder God as more need to be on their knees.
So many who have no Savior, are dying in helpless pleas
For their plea is for a messenger, the one called out by Your Son.
It is that one they need to hear Your word from and their broken pieces may become one.
God is calling so many to be transformed to his way.
Oh the call is echoing but Lord few will pray.
The world is a broken cistern crying for its potter.
Lord we need your hands and feet assembled, your body working, restoring the clay with Your living water.
As the call rings out will there be one on their knees to hear?
On our knees in prayer You quell our insecurity and dismiss our petty fear.

So we may minister Your Truth and
carry out Your great commission.
Oh lord it is obtainable to all with open ears, and
have not committed prayer to omission.
A call none will chase as it is risky and calls
us out of the norms,
to reach across our streets, our neighborhood and
our dorms.
It is a call of anguish, a call to step out in faith.
out of the boat into a raging ocean as Peter we will
follow what your voice saith.
Pray without ceasing as the troubles will never cease.
We are powerless without God's hand and His peace.
Oh the call is there just reach out to it on your knees.
For what the world has to gain is a lost soul and
judgment only Your Son can appease.
Pray without ceasing, pray as it is the Spirit's power.
For we need Your anointing oil and Your strength
and righteousness on us to shower.
Lord may these last lines be my prayer, a prayer for
more to pursue a call none will chase.
For apart from Your holy identity freely given, they
are worthless accidents, condemned to death
without grace.
Is it done for them? Lord don't let it be,
if they won't chase the call, call out to me.
Is it done for them? Lord don't let it be,
if they won't go for You Lord send me.

To Die Is Gain

To live is Christ to die is gain.
let these words be my life's refrain.
Let Your love be a constantly repeating chorus.
As Jesus Christ my Savior has died and paid the debt
for us.
Counting all things as loss for the
excellency of the knowledge of Jesus Christ my Lord.
Your knowledge has cleaned my heart and it has
severed my brokenness with a mighty sword.
But in pieces, You did not leave me alone.
Your Son, my Savior has set me by His side before
the throne.
Forever a part of Your priesthood a Saint,
You call me by name;
even when my darkness and sin has continued to
mock your glory and leave me in shame.
The value within one life in Your eyes, one cannot
explain.
as Your Son hung on the tree, the
sacrifice was not sent in vain.
Live Victorious, free from guilt, forever mine Jesus
cries,
as the sweat and blood drip from His brow
and tears roll from His eyes.
It is finished, it is done, Father forgive
them for they know not what they do.
Oh Lord in the shadow of Your cross with
a blood covered heart I follow you.

You suffered the brutal death that was sentenced to me.
In your blood soaked swaddling clothes my
life is wrapped in liberty.
Oh but the grave it did not hold you, not a day or
hour more,
than what You had promised, as I now stand
restored!
Forever Alive, living in me, let this be my morning
cry!
As my sin and darkness encamp around me and
drag me down to die.
In my bloody pit, your arm reaches out to bear,
The depravity of my soul and the depths of my
despair.
You have clothed me in white robes, cleaned my
wounds,
providentially set me on my feet.
For Your cross and resurrection, my
unqualified soul and raging doubt it did defeat.
To live is Christ oh to die what a gain.
Lord Your presence is precious to me as it is lovingly
breaking away my heavy chains.
Anoint my head with oil, let my cup be overflowed.
For Your lovingkindness is desired and your
seed of truth in me may it be sowed.
A life in You, what physical thing could I compare.
For it is greater than the depths of the ocean and
more majestic than the universe above the air.
Your great name resounds in my head, Your Son's
even

greater as He sits on his throne.
Lord in my feeble mind and weak walk with You
remind me that I am known.
By your omniscient thoughts, and Your sacrificial love
imparting grace.
Lord draw me closer, spark a fire in my soul
that my hands and feet will chase.
To know my spots are precious, my flaws are no
longer beheld in Your sight.
Let this truth empower my walk and Your pursuit of
the broken be my fight.
oh God, your all I long for in weakness and in all,
You are all I need.
To live is Christ to die is gain, may Your life,
oh God, be the life that I feed.
oh God, your all I long for in struggle and in all,
You are all I need.
May Your given life ,oh God, be the life that I feed
⍰

Meet me on the Mount

Meet me on the mount it's the call the climber
received.
Try as he may the climber has been deceived.
Meet me on the mount it has been the climber's
heart cry.
Try, try harder, try harder the climber will surely die.
Meet me on the mount; meet me at
a standard I have set forth.
It is from the mount of the most high the
true one that abides in the north.
Meet on the mount, I know this but
I cannot attain no matter how hard I travail.
I meet failure after failure with condemnation
as a boisterous wind into a sail.
Meet me at the mount, I cannot, I will not
I have fought far too long.
I cannot summit this trial as lamentation
and sorrow is my song.
Meet me on the mount, the call is distant
but still distinctly heard.
Who does this voice think I am
I cannot meet him at his word?
I cannot adhere to this challenge,
I cannot hold my grip on the snow covered rocks.
I cannot leap over the crevasses, my fear and
inadequacy has me in chains with great locks.
Meet on the mount, the standard was set
it will not move for me I must adhere.

I cannot, I will not, I guess the avalanche of fate
has for me what I deserve, I fear.
A life without direction, a life without a voice,
this is what I have to face.
For I cannot meet You on the mount and
I cannot continue at this pace.
The voice dies out; the call is diminished to an empty
silence
 I must now go my own way down this mount
to its base to the start.
It is there I must begin again and find the desires of
my heart.
I do not need the standard, I do
not need the commandments set long ago.
I have been here long enough to know
what is best and let my discipline go.
Meet me on the mount, the call arrives again
but is closer than ever before.
It is then I see a man at the base waiting by the
oceans shore.
This is not he, the one that called me to
such a high standard and expectation.
This cannot be, I have worked too hard for
this in great turmoil and desperation.
He cannot be at the base, the one that
calls must be on the top.
For what is a life without effort of my own or
lessons learned as I rise and drop?
Meet me at the mount, the words proceed
from the man I see at the base.
This cannot be I cry, I am a failure, I have done

nothing I am a disgrace.
The man walks to me as I weep, as I
fall with all my gear and supplies.
He takes my hand and brushes off the weighty
snow and says rise.
Head low, eyes full of tears, my heart broken in
defeat.
The man takes me to a dwelling where
he removes my boots and washes my feet.
I can have no part of this, I have done nothing, and I
must go out and do more.
Do not treat me kindly when I am worthless
unable to meet the one who called out before.
For the one that called before, my work is required
so
it must be right and just.
Let me be, let me go and take on this mountain I
must, I must.
The man just washes my feet, intently listening but
not seeming to care.
He finishes and looks at me and says go,
no one will meet you there.
But the voice, the call, the standard, I must try, I
must work,
there must be reward for those that strive.
The man shakes his head, and replies there is no
reward for
those who fight to stay alive.
For the man that keeps his life will lose it and the
man
that loses it will find life indeed.

The call was from the top, but it is here in humility
and meekness I will lead.
For no man reaches the top apart from me the only
guide.
No climber no matter how stout or qualified has ever
reached the caller without me at his side.
Go your way, but if you do not have a part with me
you will eternally fail and fall.
Stay here with me and I will take you to
the One that gave the call.
Meet me on the mount, the principle is
high but the cost is low.
For those that let the guide at the base wash their
feet will have no limit to how high they can go.
Never again alone, forsaken they will never be.
They will be able to traverse the depth, the heighth
and the width of the mount forever free.
Meet me at the mount may this message be in your
heart.
Blessed are those that meet me in brokenness at the
start.
For the race is not to the swift, nor to the strong.
It is not about those who are right or those who are
wrong.
For great is the reward for those that forsake their
efforts and give their walk over to me their guide.
Blessed are those that are lowly, and
seeking righteousness at my side.
Blessed are the meek for they will surely
see the kingdom above.
For those who have forsaken their life to meet me

find fountains of grace and love.
I am more than the guide; I am the way,
the truth and the life.
I am that I Am the one who called
you out from your toils and strife.
I dwell at the top setting a standard no man can meet.
I dwell at the bottom where I wash the humbled feet.
I dwell in between calling out to
those who endlessly attempt and fight.
I dwell on the mount, but none will
overcome it without my might.
Blessed you are, the man says to me as he leads the way.
Blessed you are, for you have met the Lord today.
Meet me on the mount, I will meet you there.
For the law has been fulfilled, and you can rest in my care.
My yoke is easy, my burden is light.
What gain is there if a man gain the world
and lose his soul in the fight.
Blessed are those that are pure in heart, I
give this to those that follow me.
Meet me on the mount of Grace where
you are eternally free.
?

How long will You Stand?

How are the things of Esau searched out!
How are his hidden things sought up?
For when the kingdom is come unto this earth, not a
soul among you will be caught up.
Forsaken you will become, for forsaken you have left
me first.
You will cry in your destruction, but there will be
none to attend to your hunger and thirst.
For the severity of God, is not to be meddled with or
forgot.
The great tribulation will come as a desolation to all
those who never considered my Son and never gave
Him thought.
Oh sons of Esau why have you stood in the way as a
hindrance for my sons and daughters.
For thy violence against Jacob, shame shall cover
thee and thou shalt be cut off from the earth and its
waters.
Not a comfort to enjoy as all will come to pass.
Not a voice of repentance when I sent unto
you a messenger, the very last.
Do not take the call of the Lord or
his warning as something light.
For we have but a time on this earth and all
unrighteous without His blood's covering will be
judged in His sight.
For great love is covering and offered
to all those who seek to be atoned.
Written in the book of life by which by God

we will be considered and known.
Stand not in the way of sinners; abide with the world
no more.
For what the world has to offer
is coming judgment without before a great white
throne.
We all stood before the cross or at least our sin as it
was placed into each scar and wound.
Of our God and Savior, the Lamb, the Son, by which
our separation from above was pruned.
No longer apart, no longer standing by the gates of
hell,
but in between in a battle of angelic conflict given a
choice to where our life we will sell.
Two kingdoms stand, but one has stood
eternally before the fall.
The kingdom of a God, of grace, that in eternity past
took great pleasure in our creation and died for us
all.
The cross stood before time, and it still stands today.
Choose this day whom you will serve and follow his
way.
Look not upon the children of God as they become
strangers, persecuted and in the devil's destruction.
Heed unto the call of the Father that sent the Son
providing provision and simple instruction.
Confess and believe, turn your mind to
the one who has already suffered.
For there is but a short time, and an account of
unbelief that cannot be buffered;
Oh sons of Esau, Those left in the heathens rage.

Repent unto the Christ and forever be saved from
this age.
Be no longer possessed by this present world and
look unto the Father that flags of freedom are risen
and unfurled.
Be a worshipper of Yahweh, the one that redeemed
the discord between both sons.
Changing the name of Jacob to Israel, you too have a
new name with battles already won.
Come to me saith the Lord, or forever be set at
naught.
For small you will become among the heathen and
greatly despised objects of my wrath soon to be
taught.
Exalting thyself as an eagle, nest set as high as the
stars.
You are consumed and pre-occupied with the
pleasures of sin, finding comfort in destructions
scars.
Your sin will not be forgotten unless it is
covered and forgiven.
By the Son sent to die, that in victory is now alive and
risen.
This is a cry of Obadiah, the believer
speaking out to you today.
Dwell no longer in the desolation of the fall and
embrace Grace and mercy's way.
How long will you stand and believe you
can overcome your sin?
For there is a cry unto all to repent and believe
leaving the mess our wrongs have left us in.

Stand Fast in Liberty: Freedom proclaimed

Stand fast in liberty for the enemy seeks to take it
away.
Stand in freedom, flee the bondage of the day.
This is the truth you are forever free from the great
lie.
Give this day your heart to God and never die.
I marvel at how quick we run to our old bloody
chains.
When the blood is not our own,
but Christ's that broke bondage with the stains.
Why when we have begun in a work that was not our
own.
We run to the law and slavery denying
what Christ freely came to atone.
Oh foolish generation when will we realize.
We were not made to serve bondage,
but liberty with open eyes.
So quickly we wear veils, face the east blindly falling
down.
When by the blood of our Savior we were declared
free princes with an eternal crown.
Easily deceived we are when we know that we once
received what is truly right.
Reciting a dead law while carrying hatred through
life's fight.
Live in the liberty of love in bondage to none.
For the law is dead and in the liberty of Christ
all battles are won.
Do not forget the foundation of

all things and when creation was set.
For it was God and man in unity that the
prerequisite of all things was met.
So when you seek to tear down the life I have inside.
Please recall the grace and freedom that was liberally
given for us to abide.
Just as the time before where the son of promise
was born from the woman that was free.
I am not subject to your law that seeks to spy out my
liberty.
We were created equal beings with God's breathe
you and I.
The only difference stands that I have received
freeing truth and you have accepted bondage of a
lie.
Stand fast in liberty of the good news of Jesus, not
the prophet, but Christ the king forever glorified.
Choose this day who you will serve as you are not
bound to law as in Christ the fulfillment was
satisfied.
Stand fast in liberty be free from the laws strangling
hate.
As a leash upon a dog the law will
diminish your free will and seal your fate.
Christ as king of kings for He is the
only God that cares for you.
The only God that keeps your tears and does not
condemn us for what we have done or presently do.
The only God that understands our past and present
pain,
The only god that declares a life worth

living and a death with Him great gain.
Stand fast in liberty no matter what
you believe or have believed in the past.
For God so loved the world He sent His Son giving
freedom and life that forever will last.
The truth is found within the one upon the cross
crucified.
Be foolish no more for what you live
in is in a way that has died.
For the just live by faith, son of Abraham stop living
by sight;
for your father was counted righteous not by works
but by faith in the True God free from the law's
might.
Turn your fervent prayers to the
One God who came to set you free.
For a life of bondage to law manifest nothing
spare hate with an eternal fee.
The culture and priest zealously affect you but not
well.
For Zealotry misplaced in the letter of the law, will
bring destruction beyond what stories could tell.
For your soul was made for freedom, not to be
subject to a standard we can never meet.
The standard was set before our time and was
settled when Jesus Christ took his seat.
Walk in His Spirit for in it your zealotry will be rightly
placed;
zealous to love those around you and zealous to
proclaim a judgment that has been erased.

I write this letter with much to say, knowing it is
contrary to what you may believe.
I only ask for the best from you that is not performed
but freely received.
For I am but one of many trophies, as you can be of
Grace.
Accept Jesus as Christ your savior as He desires to
be with you face to face.
Let no man or bondage affect you for a step towards
Christ as it is processed will forever be sealed.
For upon Calvary's cross all sin was dealt with and
our souls wounds were forever healed.
Stand in liberty for it is truly just a step of faith away.
For whosoever seeks righteousness
will find Christ is the only way.

I Am a Helpless one

I am the helpless one begging on the street
I am the woman at the corner, looking
for a man to meet
I am the invalid having an issue within my blood
I am the most wretched of all, the
one you missed in the flood
I am the helpless one for I have
no reference of who I am
I am the one lost from the fold,
I am the missing lamb
I am the helpless one, why do you
not seem to hear my cry
I am the one without hope as everything I have
put hope in has died
I am the hopeless one, my ambitions are a cloud
fading with the rain.
I am the one you ignore on the street as
my body is overwhelmed with inner pain.
I am the one that needs, the one that
is endlessly dependent on others
I am the one that has no family,
no sisters, no brothers.
I am the one without a people,
an outcast from the chosen few
I am the one waiting at the well, waiting to
see what you will do
I am nothing but what my shortcomings
and failures can describe
I am these things as these are the

names the voices of others prescribe
I am the one caught in adultery;
I am the one expecting death by Your hands
I am the one that has failed to adhere to the law and
all the sacred commands
I am the helpless one that many
have said must help myself
What do I have to help other than this
broken life upon time's shelf
I am all these things if not more, but your words,
your hands they are gentle and don't judge
How can you be just and look on me with
mercy when for the law I would not budge?
Condemn me now, end this cycle of my great despair
For no form of rules could ever restore who
I am or even come close to repair
For I am the helpless one, a spotted,
blemished lamb before the spotless king
But as a shepherd you have shown me grace and
have renounced death's sting
You see me as I am, but have
spoken to me as I am not.
For what has my life been other than what others
have proclaimed or judgment others have sought?
You say I am the reason you are here,
you say I am not condemned anymore
You say that is finished, but how can I leave who I
am, the helpless one, broken and poor
You say you have waters of life, waters that
have no need to be replenished
You say I can live in these waters and be

proclaimed clean and unblemished
You say where are your accusers,
 I do not condemn you, now go sin no more
You have shown me a character, a love and
grace that I cannot ignore
Please say more, Your words are precious in these
days I dare not let a word fall to the ground
Speak more to me about this living water,
about this mercy that I have found
Speak about Your kingdom, about your love for me
from before the world's foundation
Speak to me about who I am in Your sight, who I will
become, what I can do among the nations
You speak so highly of me, these words they
are too great and health to me
You speak to the helpless one, the one caught in sin
and set them free
Friend of publicans and sinners, be my friend, I have
none with words like yours
For none have I met, have such beautiful things to
say of me, or have such instruction
leading to open doors
For when You speak to me, I feel
my heart is set free from its defined chains;
From the person I am, to a person that I cannot
relate to or even associate with my name.
You give me a new name, one that is
defined by what You say
I am the helpless one that has found the Savior, or
rather He found me as a sheep gone astray

Accepting me as His own, though I was a vain woman
at the well, an exposed woman
before many accusers
A helpless beggar, a sinner that was
at the mercy of self-righteous abusers
I was the helpless one, but I am this no more
I am now one that has been personally met
by the Savior,I am the restored
I was the one begging on the street,
but this also I am not
I am now the woman at the
well that Jesus desperately sought
I was the woman at the corner
waiting for a man to meet
I am now the woman with oil in
my hair washing Jesus feet
I was the helpless one, the one
that God missed in the flood
I am now the redeemed, equipped and
able made perfect by Christ's blood
I am no longer what others define me to be
I am no longer my circumstance;
I am no longer my degree
I am no longer the woman caught in adultery or
the woman at the well
I am no longer the broken heart, I am no longer
the one that fell
I am no longer the blind outside the city,
no longer the dead one in the grave
I am no longer what the world can offer,
but what the Lord has saved

I am no longer the accused, for I have been
forgiven by grace from above
I am the one now resting on Christ, of
whom Jesus greatly loved
?

House Of Grace

New to the job site, I am accepted into the daily fray
Building this house, this massive structure one
that is promised to stay
I make some friends, They introduce me to the
master
They say stay with him, watch him as
you will grow and learn faster
I admit the builder was skilled he designed the
structure we are to place
He found the foundation stone, set it immovable in
its place
He sculpted precious stones for the walls, and used
them as his building base
He led me through the inner workings and
explained that this is a house of grace
It did not seem too special, its appearance was
appealing but not ornate
The builder described it as a masterpiece, but it
stood among the poor and not among the great
Its structure would surely stand, as it was built upon
a rock
Its cornerstone was the strongest I have seen and its
walls strongest of the stock
I wondered as the master loved it, he created it and
planned to dwell within it as his secret place
But I did not see it as anything great, it was just a
strong home not a house of beauty or grace
I carried on with my job building more
houses around the master's prize

more and more it was surpassed by design,
but its strength none could realize
For when storms came, the others were torn up
uprooted foundations piles of rubble by the end of
the day
But the house of grace stood strong and
none could replicate its way
Devastated by loss, my work fell through I was
jobless without provision and a place
My home was in my work, but now it is
homelessness I must now face
displaced many times, turned down, unskilled and
labeled a hopeless case
I do not deserve this mess I cry, I am capable
and still in this race
I power up and go, pushing through the lines,
working, I will bring sunshine to this rain
But I find it is ever more hopeless and my efforts are
in vain
I am met by a stranger, he speaks of
this man that was calling out my name
the stranger said, the man had a plan for me and
could provide riches and fame
I ran to this man, he had a place in the development
where my work once stood
He gave me great opportunities, restored my way
and affirmed everything was good
He aimed to rebuild, restructure everything,
bring order to the place
But he demanded destruction, compromise,
and sought to deface

Spoiled by his schemes I followed this man
and did all his deeds
I felt miserable as his ethics were flawed and he built
his empire upon lust and greed
He rallied a following, and marched over to the
master's place
For through it all there still stood the house of grace
Its walls still strong, its foundation sure
Its master still indwelling its integrity strong and pure
The stranger demanded its destruction
as it was affront to his land
But no tool could damage its walls and no machine
would complete his demand
I resort to step inside, talk to the master and discuss
the terms the law has placed
One must pay the price, the cost to dwell in the
house of grace
The master responds to the demand, but request
that I would stay
He says, "the price will be paid and the stranger
will no longer have his way"
"His empire is vast", I reply you cannot stand
against it as it is too strong and unjust
The master just shakes his head and responds his
world is dust
He tells me the appointed time is coming
where the system will fall
He will return to the house of grace that stands,
and he will lead us all
unworthy to dwell, unworthy I cry as
my work is vain it is a crime and disgrace

The Master answers, no worries for
you now dwell in the house of grace
You will never deserve it, but for you the price is paid
Rest in this house for its foundation is eternally laid
Its dimension is endless it will be filled with those
you tell
For the hurting and hopeless like you I designed this
house for them to dwell
It comes at no cost, as I already stood to pay its price
Just tell those searching, it is finished ,
dwell in the house of grace built by Christ
I was crucified in love towards you, I was revealed to
you in this house's construction
Your friends led you to me, you saw me but
your heart was set on destruction
But have no fear, For in this house there is every
provision
No law can separate you from my love and in my
presence will there be no division
Rest now in this house of grace for in it
my righteousness I impart
I must go now, I will be with you, remember
I chose to do this part
I look outside the house to see Jesus stand
before the stranger and be slain
In this display I feel my burdens lifted and
I am relieved of guilt's pain
Surely This is my Savior, my master from the start
Building a house of grace in the confines of my heart

I Am Here

I am here ears open reading your word
I am here receiving grace, acting in utterance
so it's heard
I am here ready and willing to partake and witness
your power
I am here ministering your truth, so souls
may be saved this hour
I am here with hands empty not
a qualification to my name
I am here so that Your name is made great
and your glory receives the fame
I am here as your apostles in time before
I am here to step in your footsteps and
travel to that distant shore
I am here, because you have called me out, set me
aside, given me value and Great purpose.
I am here to speak profound things to others as your
word goes deeper than the surface.
I am here to be your vessel for thy names sake
I am here because your grace and
love I dare not forsake.
I am here according to the gift of the grace of God
given unto me by the effectual working of His power
I am here because if I was not I would be
Without Identity, damaged, destroyed and devoured
Keep me here as I know that I
Cannot stand here in my own capacity
It is your strength I draw from,
And your loving zeal for my tenacity

Preserve my way in your way as the hymn
I am prone to wander
Keep me in your word, in your spirit, and in
meditation of your truth may I ponder
The way you rescued me from the darkness and how
you desire to do the same for others
Keep me here Oh Lord, for the sick, the outcasts, the
orphans and for the widowed mothers
I am here completely because it is here only that I
can stand
For nothing will change in this world and this life, if I
do not commit it to your hand.

Rebuild Our Temple, Give us Your Word

This is an account of my trouble; this is an account
of all my grief
In an occupied kingdom, an outcast among a culture
unknown;
in a kingdom of my enemies under the rule of a
corrupt throne
You have a divine plan to bring back your law and
send your presence as relief
Relief of your mercy, to a remnant that has lost all its
hope
Among the walls and mountains of my trouble, your
grace leaves a stronghold, a secure line, a ladder of
anointed rope
Help this nation turn from the strange wives, and
idols deep within their hearts
Restore us wholly, restore our bodies, ours spirits
separated from you, our deepest parts
Use the occupation of destruction be
overturned by your loving favor
Favor underserved, for thy name's sake show
us the glory of your grace
and its everlasting essence and savor
Reveal your word to me, reveal it among the ruins of
my soul
Give me thy name; remind me of your deliverance,
your salvation that made me whole
Why must it take ruin to realize our strongest traits?
Why must I go through such deep pain and suffering
to understand just how long my savior waits?

Why must the heathen rage, as I,
your son declines in destruction?
Why must there be silence in my wanton searching,
and such conviction among loving instruction?
My soul is my greatest enemy; your word is all I need
to overcome its raging strength
Help me find it in my rubble, bring your health, bring
back hope restore my faith.
In the midst of our rubble, there is an invested holy
word.
Within our fallen souls and spirits, the word of God is
patiently waiting to be found and clearly heard.
Be still as He calls, listen for the survivor among
our wrecked life
For this survivor paid it all to keep us alive and
overcome our plaguing strife.
Using the circumstance of the evil,
the decrees of wicked kings
God's word and presence is established strong in our
hearts to proclaim victory and let freedom ring.
Save us from our present bondage,
save us LORD God, hear the remnants cry.
Number your people searching for you, meet us in
our ruined city, let your temple be restored and
your praises be lifted high.
Higher and higher, let the voices of your people rise,
the meek remnant of a once strong nation proclaim
That there is none like you God, no one greater in
the entire world, No one with such an excellent
name!

Revive me today; know my name as I solely seek
your way above the ways I have tried before
Lead me to your living scriptures, fill me with your
message, and open the once closed doors
Build your presence in my heart and soul,
rebuild these broken walls
Build your spirit in your people, lift us up among
our many failures and great falls
Rebuild these broken walls, rebuild it
through circumstance's decree,
for there is no greater love than this, rebuilding the
broken temple when it was I who tore it down upon
that tree.

Reflections

Lord I look upon my life as a map that is yet to be
established and purposefully drawn out
A map with lands of great trials to come,
a map with islands of solitude,
a map with deserts plagued with drought
A map unfinished as time is still unfolding
its depths and directions
A map of my life, a map of reflections
Help me read this map, help me find what is hidden
within its many terrains and oceans
Help me lord find my way in the lands with no sun
shining, no north stars to direct my motions
I find that what is mapped out, is all working within a
larger map that you hold above
A map that contains my tainted map of life, but
integrates it into the most grand of all maps in love.
How can my free will be exercised within what I only
see as constraints in your word?
How can I explore and make an adventure of life and
experience the things unseen and unheard?
I tread now in a valley, carefully mapped out as
it is a land of toil and with turns that lead to deadly
snares.
It is here I see the constraints perceived before are
the signatures of a Holy God loving me in my valleys
and demonstrating that he cares.
I find there is constraint, but viewing these as grace I
see there is abounding liberty to come;

as I map out the valley quickly without error and can move onto the pastures and mountains enjoying the fullness of freedom.

My map of life can grow and stretch far among the many maps of other's existence.

As I have a compass, navigator, and watchman with faithfulness and graceful persistence.

My map is far from finished, but I am thankful for what is now there.

It is a map with many valleys but among these there are great oceans, pastures, and mountains reminding me that I was never far from Your care.

Anxious to see its fullness, I am hopeful to see its impact on those who follow in its directions behind.

I am amazed to see such a beautiful map that is a light among human kind

It was not always this way it was once a constrained fragment complex as a maze.

But among this complexity came a simple but mighty compass that led me out of the pits haze.

Finding lands unexplored and lands still standing without claim

The navigator then sent me out to the uncharted places and left them for me to name.

It is in the uncharted land that I realized that I now had a fervent and vigilant watchmen watching and waiting when I would wander into the pits and caves. And when I had all but given up, I would hear His still small voice directing me toward the roads that he had paved.

Taking note not to wander away again from the trinity of truth and pure direction.

I found that my map was being developed for others use and many were taking note of its eases and complexions.

My life is but a map for those willing to search for its connection to the map above.

My life is but a reflection of the map of God's great sovereignty and unfailing love.

They will not need to dig within its contents or explain its errors or shortfalls.

They only need to look upon the cross, the compass that leads to the navigator that calls.

It is finding the great navigator that all men and their maps will be truly set free.

For This is my Savior, my light upon my feet, the one who has taken my map of reflection and has redefined me.

Unlock the Mind

I am fallen in my countenance, blinded by what I can see.
I am separated from truth and filled with vain knowledge and empty philosophy.
What is the meaning of life, the question that so many not dare ask in honesty.
We stand with open minds but no space for truth as we are overtaken by the current of activity.
This is my life, my mind is open but its reception is filtered only to please my emotional ears.
Receptors inspiring me with deep questions that will have me pursuing answers for endless years.
Honestly I am contrary, a living paradox and an offense to sound rationality.
As I refuse to accept just the simple truths in defense of keeping my individuality.
But who am I without truth, who am I and what can truly define a man aside from true reality?
For the facts and depths of truth are intrinsically set in a footing that none can move within mortality.
A foundation rooted within reason, within design, and the cosmos of the sky.
A foundation that is progressive and immutable, a foundation that lived eternal and chose to die;
A foundation that includes all the facilities and complexities of who we are, but is somehow far beyond.

It is a foundation that goes further than the substance of the blood and the chemistry within evolution's pond
It is a foundation set so deep, it is a black hole, one that goes beyond matter and energy's confines.
A foundation that is eternal without question, and a foundation that demands to be no less than divine. . .
If divinity is the answer, what depth is there then and what questions are there to answer now?
When it is divinity, what more can I do other than blindly accept and bow?
Oh feeble minded we are when we dismiss the God of eternity as being something less than par.
For in the knowledge of the divine, there is a Character to know and a grand design that explains who we are.
Think no more, that having a Creator God is the death of intellectual pursuit and curious behavior
When there is an invitation to know an eternal being, an everlasting wealth of knowledge and a Loving Savior.
Take a moment and truly think, what original thoughts are truly your own?
Take a moment with the God who created you and realize new revelations are just waiting to be sown.
For in the knowledge and revelation of God, Creator, Eternal one, uncreated but existent, unthinkable but known, Seated high above but also below as our Savior.

You have a potential in the mind that can alter who you are and easily adjust your perception and once immovable behavior.

Before the mountains, thou art God. What more do we need to search for apart from this truth so simple, but endless in its facets and perfections.

This is a truth that can alter the world, and can alter the inner mind's ponderings and reflections.

Men of reason do not dismiss the simple; do not deny the opportunity as it has the potential to change all things for true good.

The simplicity of Christ can take you on a journey founded in truth that will look where no other men would.

Hear the Psalmist cry, Hear the Christian inspired by an eternal living God.

View divinity no more as a despotic leader viewing your life and waiting with an iron rod.

For God is much more, much more when He is added into the overarching context of life.

A God that imparts wisdom to the searching, and comfort to those caught in strife.

This is more than simple truth, it is truth with many attributes to be studied, examined and defined.

It is the truth that God greatly desires to challenge you in love and unlock the egresses of your mind.

Woe is Me

Woe is me for I am undone, standing before the one I will call my Savior, The one in whom the final victory is won.

Why me, why here, among a nation most unclean? Why the wandering in this maze of life with an end unseen?

I have a purpose; it was lost as I entered this world with blood corrupted. A blood tainted by generations of sin, and a blood that holds evil with depths unknown.

A cursed blood and a rebellious nature, a blood that has enmity towards your throne,

Why with such evil, is there a light of revelation proceeding from Your Holy word with glory too majestic and beautiful to be revealed?

Why shed such light into my dark soul where there is only wickedness and evil concealed?

Why is such glory wrapped in swaddling clothes, why such glory of at a cross?

Why sacrifice such glory of a pure blood descended from High to pay the cost for all who are lost?

Woe is me for I am undone.

How can you be coming with such humility to serve your enemy and call them daughters and sons?

Depart from me for I am unclean and dwell in the land of unclean lips.

I cannot stand here and accept such a revelation and be declared right alongside the light that no moon or darkness can eclipse.

If it is here that you must dwell who then shall you send?

For there is not a man to stand within the gap, or any righteous that when tempted will not bend.

We are pliable and fluid, we are as fickle and wandering as the wind and the raging sea

How can an issue of blood be redeemed by one, and how can by one all be set free?

For it pleased the Father to bruise the Son, for by His stripes are we healed and by His sacrifice all those divided and decimated by sin can once again be made one.

Why does such judgment have to fall on one that is so great?

Why not judge the world and create all things new, with all things in order and in line?

Why must you show grace to the fallen dust that resist all that is Holy and divine?

Woe is me for all is undone. A virgin shall bear forth a child and all things can be redeemed and made new.

Ushering in an age that was a mystery to the ages, but an age of grace where your love will reach out to the whole world and desperately pursue.

To pursue ones like me, unclean and on course for destruction and dismay, How can this be you pursue the ones that surround me and the ones who have lost their way?

This is my Savior, the one who says it was His great pleasure to redeem and reconcile those who have pushed Him far off

My Savior who took the nails of hatred and bore the sin of all and persisted as many mocked and scoffed. I cannot stand before this revelation. I cannot walk within its gravity and truth, for I am but a servant, a wayward prophet, an unclean priest.

How can I be among your cherubim and angelic host when I am among the least?

How is it that you have purified my lips with coal that is severe and sweet?

You have sent your message to the stammering mouths and unsure feet.

Woe is me for am no longer who I once was before. You have taken the impurity of my life and have called me out for more!

You have called me to be more than what my nation could perceive, more than what I could ever fathom or pursue.

You have called me to be more than my ability, and do more than what I could ever do.

You have called me to greatness that is empowered by none but You!

Who then shall You send, ask no more I plea, let no man live without this truth and die.

Who else is there with such revelation of truth and freedom but I? Send me, Send me I cry.

Send me for more need to know what I have seen: the truth of the end, an age of ultimate judgment and inescapable severity.

The truth that there is a messiah who died on a
cross, and there is a coming age of eternal peace and
prosperity.
What if the revelation of God, is all I will ever need?
What if instead of trying to figure my life out I could
look to the one and only incorruptible seed?
What more do we need, than a revelation
or vision from above?
What are we seeking beyond the cross where we
witnessed an unfathomable act of grace and love?
Woe is me for I have lost sight of what is truly holy
and important to my life.
I allow so many burdens that are not mine to bear
cause endless struggle and strife.
Please forgive us Father, for we know not what we
do or what we should cherish.
We forget that the cross stands still within our hearts
proclaiming none should perish.
Purify our lips, purify mine above all as they are often
unused and silent.
Lips hiding a tongue untamed that is raging evil and
violent.
Let my mouth be purified as Isaiah's lips were
restored.
Help me build the bridges my words have burnt and
let my words be a light that wayfaring souls can find
truth in and restfully be moored.
I am undone by your revelation; I am awestruck
within its all-encompassing grace.
I have stood within the Holy of Holies, past the veil
that was torn before my Savior face to face.

Send me I cry, send me for who else is there with such a personal encounter with grace and what is truly free?
Send me as I am yours, seeking those you have sent your son to save as they cry, woe is me.

Keep what has been committed: To a Faithful friend

Oh men of faith keep what has been committed.
For in your heart grace was formed and fitted.
Man of faith, know that within grace there is a peace
that will never end.
Know this day that a relationship found in Christ
will eternally be a friend.
Keep what has been committed, but do not try to
hold it on your own.
For the power that keeps you and I is the power
of the lamb seated upon the throne.
Keep what has been committed, sound words,
sound teachings and a mind ever stable.
Know the truth is nothing apart from Jesus crucified,
resurrected the third day and now alive; do not be
given to long tales or fables.
Let no man despise thy youth, let all thy conversation
be filled with love and purity.
For invested in you is great and powerful truth, you
have a sound doctrine that is health and stability.
For in knowing the great oracles of the Savior above
Your life will be filled with great compassion
and an undeniable love.
Keep what has been committed study as a
workman that needeth not be ashamed.
For what can man do to you when life eternal is
raging within your soul as a great lion untamed.
For godliness with contentment is great gain.
For what money cannot buy, in your heart you have
attained.

I know what has been in you is great faith
as your family before.
I can only dream of the difference you will make as
Christ leads you through the next open door.
Keep what has been committed, never waver or
be overcome by doubt.
For what can the world offer you aside from a
broken life and a long season of drought?
As Christ has loved you so greatly I write this to you,
a passionate disciple I love you the same.
For in Christ I see nothing but unlimited potential
and heavenly glory and fame.
Adorned with the treasures of heaven, their
beauty none can explain.
Within your heart I see a great magnificence that the
world cannot temper or contain.
Your heart is on fire with great love, I beseech
you don't let the lie quench its heights.
For among the many witnesses of grace I see you the
brightest of lights.
Keep what has been committed as so many will try to
steal it away.
With eloquent speech and teachings they will waver
your faith and cause you to sway.
Don't leave truth; it is all you need in this life, I know,
as I have seen life without.
Chief among the unrighteous, I was filled with anger,
shame and endless self-righteousness and self-
doubt.
For in the flesh, what can we hope to see achieved

For in the spirit there is eternal life that is freely given and easily received.
Keep what has been committed for it is the only way, I say this in verity.
For there is no other gospel apart from Jesus Christ's that has such grace on display in great clarity.
Apart from grace what more are we other than sinners most wretched and wicked in heart.
Keep what has been committed for it is what will purify you and give you a fresh a start.
Be instant to preach, apt to teach in and out of season.
For there are many without these sound sayings living a life without purpose and without reason.
Keep what has been committed for it has been committed despite your blindness.
For it is Unfailing, faithful, ever renewing your strength and saturated in God's lovingkindness.
God has loved thee with an everlasting love, giving his only Son, a divine sacrifice upon a tree.
We receive redemption from our own understanding as we are imputed true righteousness and purity.
Keep what has been committed fight the good fight of faith in my stead.
Walk by the faith you have seen before you and follow what is written and what the Lord has said.
For in you I see a blameless bishop, worthy of the ministry, and a trophy of grace upon the heavenly shelf.
For you have counted others above thee and put aside thyself.

Keep what has been committed for
I see nothing apart from Christ in you.
Dream beyond what is seen as nothing can limit
what you can accomplish or do.
For in Christ there is a power that none can deny.
There is a truth crying within that dismisses every lie.
There is a hope as in grace we are accepted wholly as
one of God's own.
There is strength amidst all weakness, amidst all our
failures of which we are prone.
There is a peace beyond understanding, a rest no
noise can disrupt.
An identity in Christ eternally stable, that none can
taint or corrupt.
Keep what has been committed for God counts you
as His own Son.
God is drawing us ever closer to Him, as He is the
Father that pursues us close even when we run.
He is ever with us in our struggle, ever teaching us
the sound way.
Christ gives us new strength to live by and new
mercies every day.
Keep what has been committed for the words
engrafted in thee are life.
For what word in the world can pierce our very souls
and save us from our strife?
What word can purify our hearts, remove guilt
or lead with such uprightness?
What word can reveal truth among our
shortsightedness?

What truth is there apart from grace, apart from a
God that jealously pursues us in divine love?
What word is so inspired, and what truth is there
that has the breathed life from above?
Keep what has been committed I can't state this
concisely with urgency or in its fullness sufficiently.
For what is there but the truth of grace? The truth,
that God who loves us, also knows us omnisciently.
Knowing this truth that the foundation of our Savior
standeth sure and true. We have a foundation that
will stand immovable and loves in spite of all we
profanely do.
Keep what has been committed for there are
volumes of it to learn and continually grow.
For I have fought the good fight, I have finished the
course I have kept the faith, Now it is your time to
go.
Go display a life that pours out grace and takes in the
weak and poor.
Go forgive those that have hurt you and love your
enemies more and more.
Go and teach the sound doctrine of which
I have given you in part.
Go study to show thyself approved, a workmen that
needeth not be ashamed or walk heavy in heart.
Go assist the widows, take in the widows that are
widows indeed.
Go live a life that has no explanation outside of what
Christ has done in times of great need.
Go full of joy lead a quite peaceable life in godliness
and honesty.

Go live a life of divine appointment in meaning and in all modesty.
For this is good and acceptable in the sight of God our Savior; that many will come to know of His great grace from your humility and anointed behavior.
Keep what has been committed let no man despise thy youth.
For in your heart there is an eternal fire I see, burning with love and great truth.

Faith Standing In the Power

"That Your faith should not stand in the wisdom of
men, but in the power of God" I Corinthians 2:5
Faith standing in the power as you have
called me to Your Name.
Faith in the knowledge of You and
proclaiming Your Glory and Your Fame.
Faith standing sure girded with Your word of Truth
and Light.
Faith immovable as no man could withstand
or contest Your might.
Faith alone in Christ, not in the wisdom or the
schemes of man.
Faith, the ability to move forward to where no one
else can.
Faith in Your power, because in nothing else will we
be free.
Faith knowing your power created and sustains what
we see.
The substance of things hoped for, the
evidence of things not seen or perceived
Lord it is Faith in You that I count on and on Your
forever strong shoulder I rest and receive
Forever on the throne, Your power is eternal.
Faith in the power thereof; it is Your truth that must
be made internal.
Indwelling forever, convicting my corrupt flesh and
damaged soul.
Faith in Your power as it is this power
that has made me eternally whole.

The Song and Faith

Faith, faith what a calling and what a cry
Faith a call to believe my loving savior lest I die
A call to be healed, a call to be renewed
A call to love others and a call
to be loved and eternally pursued
Pursued by God above and cultivated in His grace
Faith the ability to see beyond the veil and
meet Jesus face to face
Where has faith gone, when did I ever attain or
acquire,
A longing for God and a heart soft
to the Spirit driven by consecrated desire?
My gaze has met the cross, its healing power
I cannot comprehend or describe
I know in looking towards my Savior crucified,
it was then my faith came alive
Can these bones live? Only You my Savior know
And only you can take the condemned seed
I am and make it grow

There is a song, that is sung and within
each man audible but unheard
It is a song uniting all creation, with harmonies
sweet,
octaves high and low
The song that is unsearchable, indescribable,
yet is given in written and spoken word
This is a song that all have heard at one time, but has
become lost in blindness that only grows

How do I know it exist, how do I explain its
complexity in such simple verse?
The truth is that it remains unknown in its perfection,
but in part has been rehearsed.
Heard among small factions, minorities of love,
joy and peace
People that once sang different notes and a
muddled song
but by a force of mercy have
been included in the choir to
sing the song in sweet release
A release as it is a song of freedom, a release as it is
the song of adventure and stories short and long
A release that is complete as it has defined
the right and the wrong
Forsaking all this choir has joined together in
a band unbroken in love
Embracing the song in its unity and peace and
glorifying the God above
Thank the composer thank the mind behind
such song filled with grace's power
A composer that came and gave the verse we now
sing and saved us from our darkest hour
What fire now dwells within the choirs' hearts,
what love is being shed abroad
What a song to embrace the unique nature of all
who sing and what mercy to withhold heaven's rod
May the song be sung more, may it find receptive
ears and open mouths, its echo has an ever wanton
cry
A song thirsting for more in the choir, the band,

a song calling all to come and die
Why must death bring such a beautiful song,
flowing verse, and lasting satisfaction?
It is a question that haunts all that come to sight
again, it is the question demanding reaction.
What must you do then new seer, enlightened soul?
Hold onto the song that has torn me apart or
embrace the song that will make me whole?
Let the light pierce your ears and go beyond what
eyes can see
For there is a song in the spectrums of
color proclaiming in death you will be made free.
Oh great song, I hear a new verse one written but
has yet to be manifest in the air
A verse of greater volume, perfection, a verse that
will indeed reveal the song as a whole
Oh Glory, oh light unseen, mercy and grace taking
true form releasing us from the blind songs care
Come quickly oh song, my soul longs for thee in
your perfection and glory
Complete the song that is sung among the choir,
the band, and finish time's story
Let no one be left alone, without this song and
it's coming magnificence and final solution
Saving all who were once blind and sparing
the spurned from the blind songs retribution
Let all who have ears hear, let all those who have
heard be a resonating strong choir
singing the eternal song with fervency, confidence,
and consuming fire.

Where Would I Be?

Where would I be without thee? It is a question I
dare not entertain.
It is a question that haunts my dreams, it is a
meditation that moves me to tears.
To know I would be nothing more than dust nothing
more than what my broken mind could conceive,
imagine or create out of a broken world.
If the Lord had not been at my side, I fear my story
would be one of tragedy, hopelessness and
everything vain with high cost.
I would have nowhere but my fantasy and my
unreality to escape such pain and loss.
Where would I be without thee oh Lord, do not
answer let not this meditation be more than a
journey within my mind.
For if I had not You oh Lord my God at my side,
I would not be tender to the
broken and to the bitter kind.
If the Lord had not been with me, My story would be
nothing in comparison to the society or an
other man's case.
If I had not Thee with me oh God, The mirror would
not reveal my true face.
You are my Life, You are the greatest part of
what I hold most dear.
If the Lord had not been at my side, death
would be my story and
life would be my greatest fear.

Why Must The Heathen Rage

Why must the heathen rage, why must the
unrighteous live and tread on?
I have been faithful to thy statutes God and justice I
see has not been carried out or done.
Why must the evil within my heart be something I
must carry and overcome?
Why impart a new creation when the old is still
combating for my soul?
Why sacrifice Your only begotten Son
to make me whole?
Why give me grace when I bear a broken soul?
Why must the heathen rage?
Why drive the nails through your hands?
When no one is there to take a stand?
Why does the heathen rage, why must the righteous
God bear my chains?
I find I never will be satisfied with the answers,
Lord you still faithfully supply.
You have given me life in my death and living water
in my soul's droughts.
Why must there be a battle, one that cannot be won
by carnal weapons or perceived by the natural eye?
Why must the heathen rage within my heart and the
unrighteous one be no other man but I?
Help me Receive Grace today, For it is all I
can bear in this pain.
Why Sacrifice your only Son to make me whole?
Why give me grace when I bear a broken soul?

Why must the heathen rage?
Why drive the nails through your hands
When no else would take the stand?
Why does the heathen rage, why must
my Savior bear my chains?
Lord give me grace, reveal your cross within my
heart, rescue me from this torrential rain.
For the rain weighs heavy on my back as I collect it in
Sin and death's great vats
I dare not remove this yoke as it is this yoke that has
kept me straight.
It is my good works, it is the law's weight, it is my
pride, the lie that I can do this on my own.
Lord I run faster, and faster to Grace's throne.
Why sacrifice The Lamb of God to make me whole?
Why care to receive my broken soul?
Why must you give me grace, why have you
lifted my face?
Lord as the nails were driven into your hands and
feet.
The raging heathen finally found its defeat.
Why is there no more weight, why have You
given me such grace?
Why has my Savior given me such grace?

Move Me

I have not run from your call God, By your
 grace I have drawn near.
I live within a power of your spirit, and have in this
embraced the very things and people I fear.
To the glory of your cross, not any of my own as I
have no reputation before any as all has been
stripped away.
Lord I have lost my sense of who I was, but have
found who I truly am.
I find I have become the subject of a divine love and
bought back by a broken lamb.
The words now spoken, the mind I carry, the walk I
walk I know is right before thee.
This I know as I now walk within a new man that is
not constrained by the fallen man within me.
Here is my heart, here is my life, let it be within the
potters hands to mold.
Lord let my life be the clay that can be formed and
not the dry clay that will not bend or fold.
Take my desires, my ambitions, my plans and my
doubts.
Lord give unto me your living water, refresh the dry
clay within my soul's drought.
Give me your spirit's unction, an anointing that drips
from my temple to my toes.
Let the oil saturate my life and make me a minister
unmoving and bold.
Walk with me, let your presence become my
dwelling place, and your habitation forevermore.

Let my life be set apart in a ministry of your choosing
one set to a nation never reached before.

I will not hasten from your call, Lord by your grace I
will draw near and speak.

Lead me to open hearts and strengthen mine as it is
ever broken and weak.

I will dare not mention your name, but it is a fire
burning within my bones.

Lord send me, anoint your servant, and may my
heart be made as your own.

Abide In Me

I am the true vine, ye are my branches abide in me and Life will be stable and secure.
Bear fruit as I give of thee living water, and a vine that will not be severed by circumstances shears.
Abide in me and you will see rivers of life and fountains of joy form from sufferings tears.
My Father is the husbandman, tending to the branches frail and cut off by sins weeds and tares.
Revealing the power of my cross and the reconciling power of my spirit.
Engraft to me the vine and you will be nourished, cherished and forever prized by my love.
Abide in me and you will see rivers of life and fountains of joy as you are one with my father above.
Bearing fruit from my vine, you will be more than branches but friends,disciples, and seeds to the ground.
Revealing the once lost plants, that by my ever extending reach will be fused to my vine and found.
Abide in me, for apart from me you are as a withered branch in wait of judgment's fire.
Reach out all my branches, find all those lost in the weeds of the vineyard that is my greatest desire.
For each branch found, abiding in me, the Son of God, will find life forever in eternity glorifying my Father.
A branch bound to the vine will have no need to seek anymore as I am the only way to take all plants farther.

Abide in me my children, my branches, and
 live in a joy most full.
Abide in me, be delivered, let the health from my
eternal vine be in you and fulfill the deepest desire of
your soul.

Harps in the Willows

When we remembered Zion, it was a time and a
season of great sorrow.
For my soul is in great exile and my wounded spirit
cannot move onto tomorrow.
I hang the harps among willows, I dare not sing the
song of my home or of the glory of my Savior.
I am exiled from my joy and separated from
my sanctified behavior.
My oppressor demands me to sing, demands to hear
the song of my long forgotten home.
But I find I cannot sing of such things
when I am broken within my soul.
I then encourage myself in The Lord, keeping
the the matter to my mind.
Recalling the kindness of my Savior, I then know this
exile will not overcome me and I must see
beyond the lies.
I need not hang my heart's harps among the willows,
I need not forsake the joy seated and
secure within my spirit.
Rejoice evermore, I say rejoice for my Savior has
overcome the oppressor, I hear the trumpets of
victory
and the joy is there I can feel it.
Remember the Lord, in your day of exile and trouble.
For no situation can overcome the power of God, my
God the great renovator that restores broken heart's
By the rivers of Babylon weep no more for it is here
deliverance starts.

Captive to situations no more, remember the Savior upon Calvary's cross.

Play the harps strong and sing the song of heaven, as it is finished, captives have been set free, and Jesus Christ seeks to find all who have been lost.

A Sweet Savour

We are unto God, which always causeth us to
triumph
Making manifest the savour, a knowledge and
wisdom to high and excellent beyond measure.
For God causes us to triumph through the weak
things of life. Choosing rather for us to suffer as
Christ bringing forth far greater treasure.
For in Christ, we are unto God a sweet Savour.
An offering, a surrendered life that burns brighter as
each word imparted draws us
closer to our loving Savior.
A sweet savour ever greater than before, as new
creations dying daily with each step and stride.
We are ever sweeter as we are hid in Christ and His
work ever strains our flesh and weakens Sin's pride.
A sweet Savour of death unto death that is made a
fragrance of life unto life.
Who is sufficient for these things other than the
lamb slain desiring to take fallen humanity as His
wife?
We are of much sweeter savour than any flavor
devised or framed by the world could ever form.
We are much sweeter savour to God as our lives are
as rare spices bought at the highest price.
We look to Jesus the most divine ingredient, the base
from which the fulness of all fragrance flows.
We are the salt of the earth, instruments made
useful through death, but instilling greater life.
Thanks be unto God causing us to

triumph always in Christ.

Counting the dead herbs and spices of the field as His own Through His Son's burnt sacrifice.

Oh how complete, how full was the fragrance flowing from calvary's cross.

The all sufficient burnt offering, seared by Sin's flames and hung on a sacrificial hill;

Causing us to be drawn from all corners of the world, as we come we are accepted and filled.

A much sweeter Savour to our loving Father, our Savior, our indwelling Spirit with greatness from above.

A Savour of resurrected life as we are God's, made righteous through sacrifice and divine love.

The God that Holds my hand

We are as lost children, wandering about sin's great store.
We enter its atriums of pleasures and vanities and quickly lose ourselves, ever separated from God's only door.
This building started small, but as a thriving city it quickly grows.
We are all lost children drawn by its lights, music, and strong drink that freely flows.
The signs say come and stay, but as we enter they warn that we now will never leave.
We are as lost children ever wanton, needy, and naïve.
As the superstore of sin grows we are encompassed by its vast wealth.
We are as lost children without a father and in failing health.
Then a light enters the scene, at the center of the superstores great floor.
A light that is greater than the enticing lights, and far brighter than any ever before.
The door has been opened, the exit is now manifested and made clear.
The light draws us to it, but the store has become a labyrinth and a great noise deafens our ears.
We are as lost children we see the way out but are constantly distracted and drawn away.
We desire to escape sin's store, but we find on our own we cannot help but stay.

Then as a precious jewel with a thief, I am stolen
and pulled a different way.
I am captivated by a message, by a messenger
and then taken by loving hands.
I am told to stay close and take heed to simple
commands.
This is my God, the God that holds my hand showing
me the narrow road.
Leading with a gentle grasp, and relieving me of the
merchandise's heavy load.
He speaks of a greater store, one that can be
navigated and has many blessings at no cost.
He speaks of a place called heaven, and He is crying
out to find more that are lost.
We are as lost Children in great need
of a God that holds our hands.
A God of love that will direct us the right way to
escape sin's store and weaken its demands.
We are of all ages, walks, cultures and varied
histories.
Above it all God has decided to hold are hands as
children and walk us through life's great mysteries.
The mystery of sin, the mystery of a grace that
overcomes what we never could before.
The mystery of the narrow way, and the
mystery of finding heaven's door.
Oh God, how great to know you have
never left our side, or let go of our hand.
You have established us in a love divine made of
precious stone when we as children desired the
sand.

We are as Children, but you say behold my son
whom I uphold and my elect
in whom my soul delights.
You have called us out from sin's store unto
righteousness, holding our hand and keeping us in
eternal light.

Return to The Landmark

Return, Return to the old landmark set before.
Return to the Lord, return to the open door.
Do not forget, do not stray to far from
the landmarks view.
For away from the ancient landmarks, Our hearts will
stray from what is true.
Abide not with the lies of obscurity, and do
not call the grey your friend.
For destruction is what you will find in the flock
without a shepherd, and it will take you as a raging
wind.
Return, cries the Lord, return as there is
only one narrow way.
Return to the old landmark the old rugged cross, for
apart from it there is eternity to pay.
Wandering in the wilderness, wandering in the sea of
what we call the earth.
Wandering to find truth, wandering since our birth.
Direction is what God has to offer,
and Truth is what He will cry.
Wander no more oh sinner, come to the
old landmark and die.
For death is where it began and death is where it
must start once more.
Return unto the landmark of the cross, there is
resurrection life in store.
Do not let bitterness take you, do not let sin in as you
and I have the last word.
Return unto the old landmark, stop wandering

as the bird.
Return to the landmark, the landmark of light God
has placed in your heart.
For away from His plan and purpose our lives will be
consumed in our wandering before they can truly
start.

Preach.

Preach oh Believer, preach what you have
seen and heard.
Let not a jot or tittle fall to the ground, do not
neglect speaking and proclaiming one word.
For the Word of God is sharper, sharper than
anything this world has devised to divide or cut.
The word will reveal open doors to the closed off
souls, the word will open the mouths that were shut.
Preach stronger, let God's spirit reign in your soul.
Preach unto the broken world the glorious gospel,
the words that were inspired to make us whole.
Abandon the prostituting pulpits, abandon the
perverse and unclean way.
Preach the gospel pure in the streets, preach the
truth where no man will prosper or pay.
Silver and Gold have we none, but what
we have we freely offer.
Preach among the skeptics, preach among
the simple and the scoffers.
The world does not need another program, a help,
or another aid.
The world needs a preacher, who in his
heart is changed.
The world needs a witness, not an advocate, or a
priest.
The world needs a preacher, a redeemed
one among the least.
Preach ever stronger, do not let circumstance or trial
corrupt your gaze.

Keep the eyes fixed on the eternal, the Son crucified on the Cross and in three days was raised.
Let the pulpits be strong in the nations, let them catch on fire with a Holy flame.
Lord I pray the gospel may be heard louder in persecution as a raging lion that no man can tame.
May the spirit breath upon the ministries, breath upon the preachers of Your Holy Word; Lord may our tongues be like swords and our voice be like fire piercing the deaf ears in darkness. let your love be shed abroad felt and heard.

There is One

Little among thousands there is one.
A man among the millions set apart to do all
That had to be done.
A ministry and life like no other, a lamb among
the many sheep.
But there is none like this one, none that could fulfill
the promises He was bound to keep.
There is one, little among the thousands in the
streets.
Common among the people and nothing
great to their account.
But there is a potential here in this one, and a
purpose bringing great value beyond what men
could count.
Think not about the crowd, or the prevailing
voices of the wind.
Little among the thousands you may be, but God said
unto you my Spirit I send.
In a world bent on destruction, with only despair and
evil seeds to sow, the Son of God chose to die for the
little among the thousands and let His blood freely
flow.
It was not just for you, but personally Christ
has paid your price; the price for the common sin,
the price for the abundant life.
We are created for far greater, and far into eternity
our lives were supposed to reach.
Accept the One among the thousands, and let His
word have free course to train and teach.

Let the simple truth reign over the complicated lies.
Let life resonate within.
Accept the one among the thousands as He is lifted high in an eternal transaction for our sin.
For little among the thousands we are all called out to be individually true and uniquely set apart.
We are individually loved by the only one among the thousands that will comfort our heart.

Growth in Trial, Strength in Storms

Why must there be such travail in life, and such
frailty in all that we hold dear?
Why must our days be numbered, and our lives be
no more than engraved years?
Where are you God in this world, where are you in
the struggles closest to our hearts?
Why must there be silence in suffering, and
prevailing noise when peace starts?
The answer is not far from us, the righteous surely
will be delivered from their evil days.
God knows those that trust him and will deliver them
when temptation lumbers in and weighs.
Lord help me find refuge in truth, help me see you
when I am left into sufferings care.
Lord grow me in the quiet rain, lead me into prayer.
As a plant we are sown, and as a seed we are taken
by trials in wind's power.
Father deliver your sons and daughters from trouble
and the weight of that dark hour.
I find the pain does not settle, the wounds they are
present and real.
The Lord grows us in quiet rain, and strengthens our
hearts when loss is all we feel.
As my days move on, as my end year approaches
with each breath and walking stride;
The Lord grows my spirit in quiet rain, assuring me
that in Him I can eternally rest and confide.
Growing me in quiet rain, rain that weighs heavy
on the leaves but builds me at the roots.

Digging deep into my spirit, my core, guiding me in truth, my Loving gracious Savior He grows me in quiet rain.

He is ever faithful in his promises, and sacrificially taking my faults and stains.

I find there is growth in my trials, and strength in my storms.

I find each day my God is faithful to His truth, and His love effectually transforms.

My heart, my soul, my mind, the whole of who I am.

My God grows great trees in quiet rain, and creates a lion from a lamb.

How great are You God, How great are You my God to overcome my heart's crucifixion cries.

How great a love upon a cross, focused on forgiving those who have sentenced You to die.

Lord you are faithful, growing me in the quiet rain.

Let Your word be invested in my heart and your promises be evermore my confession and refrain.

I Seek Not Yours

I Seek not yours, I seek not what you do.
I seek your heart and what is eternally true.
I seek not your fame, your approbation, or your lusts.
I seek the light invested into you from above, as it is The God of heaven I forever place my trust.
I seek not your riches, I come not as a salesmen, or as an ambassador of a charity.
I seek and knock at your door, as I desire you alone and your life to be established in freedom and verity.
I seek not yours, I seek you oh lost soul.
I seek not to burden, but to lift all the unseen burdens that have you broken unaware and make you whole.
I seek out of a love anchored in the heavens above.
I seek from a hilltop, elevated on high, a hill where a cross demonstrated divine love.
I seek not yours, your time, your membership, your agreement, or your hospitality.
I seek not yours, as you have nothing to give but a life I have hung on that cross with my Savior. This is the reality.
I seek not yours and I approach in a boldness devoid of a fear of what might ensue.
I seek not yours, but you and to lead the way from eternal fire to a life that is eternally living and true.
I seek not yours, your wisdom, your intellect or argument, your emotions or your tears.

I seek not yours as I now have a spiritual life anew and the this life is all I can proclaim in joy and hear. So next time you see me, please refrain from the presumption and the many lies.

I seek not yours but you, and I seek to give the way established afore time to your heart and to open your eyes.

I Suffer

I suffer for the sake of another, I suffer with reasons untold.
I suffer to help those who may suffer, and give grace to the lost sheep of the fold.
The suffering has no origin, its purpose I cannot pinpoint or ascertain.
I am as a sheep fitted for the slaughter, and as the lamb accused and slain.
Suffering but persisting, falling but standing again.
I suffer to understand grace, and I freely will give this to my suffering friend.
Suffering is not the end, more than often it is the means.
The means to grow in grace and overcome the hurt of suffering and give this wisdom to the generations that proceed.
I suffer as a persecuted one, I suffer as a wayward Son, I suffer as a Child without a family, I suffer so that the war may be won.
But grow in the grace God has bestowed upon us. understand its depths, its heights, and its reach.
Find that grace is what pulls us through trials, and suffering is the classroom where grace may teach.
The pain will be real, its weight its digging blades will delve deeper and deeper into our souls.
But greater is the abounding grace in Christ, that when it is awakened will restore us, heal, and make us whole.

I suffered on the cross, I suffered in the grave, I suffered the weight of sin and hell.

But Grace cries my Savior, as suffering was not his home and suffering is not for us to abide in or dwell.

Sure as the rain under the clouds, and sure as the meeting man has with his grave, suffering will come unto us all in storms and in tumultuous waves.

But grace cried my Savior, and grace must we cry in our time of trouble and great need.

For grace is what will take my suffering and turn it into wisdom and a budding tree out of the rocks from the condemned seed.

I suffer to help those who suffer.

I suffer to have a word in season,

I suffer to sit in another's seat

I suffer as I know I have grace to carry me through it all, and spare me from defeat.

A Precious Stone

What is there to say apart from the fact I am greatly
blessed.
To have a Mother that loved me as I grew and
showed what God's love is more than any other.
Tending to my imperfections, while loving me still
and not sparing anything but the best.
Only God could provide such a gift, and a Precious
stone like my mother.

Loving the family, keeping it together through trails
and storms. You have been faithful through it all and
continue to nurture us all as we grow. Undefined by
the culture, raising us to be the unique and loved
ones we truly are, you are the reason our family is
set apart.
You were a light in my times of darkness and always
instilled hope and grace looking forward to who I
would become with God in sight.
In tune with God's great mind, you knew I would
overcome where I thought I could not even fight.

What is there to say apart from the fact I am greatly
blessed.
To have a Mother that loved me as I grew and
showed what God's love is more than any other.
Tending to my imperfections, while loving me still
and not sparing anything but the best.
Only God could provide such a gift, and a Precious
stone like my mother.

Now as The family is grown, your purpose and call may be obscured and maybe lost.
But precious stones are living today, able to withstand the fires of life, knowing you lived to pay the cost.
I may not be a diamond, and if I am I am still greatly flawed with imperfections life is still working out.
But a precious stone I am as I am valued by a loving mother, proud to hold me high when I would rather lie low in doubt.

What is there to say apart from the fact I am greatly blessed.
To have a Mother that loved me as I grew and showed what God's love is more than the any other.
Tending to my imperfections, while loving me still and not sparing anything but the best.
Only God could provide such a gift, and a Precious stone like my mother.

A chip off the block, the most precious stone of them all.
Refined through the fires of life along with fires of those invested into Her care.
You are a precious stone valued high above all else in my world as you are my Mother, my precious stone, prized and rare.

Roots of Righteousness

With each tree strong and tall
There is a root of righteousness establishing it all.
It is not seen, it does not seek its own.
The root seeks to establish the seed that was sown.
Though wild roots will sprout and seek vain pursuits,
The righteous will not be moved, they remain solid roots.
A man is not established by wickedness.
The man is established by a sacrifice rooted in love and tenderness.
There are roots of righteousness, set in each heart, invested by God above.
They are not moved by the wicked ways or the wandering insecurity seeking love.
Be established in what is rooted deep and stay attached to the source.
Seek no more an identity or a security that is shallow and off course.
Roots of righteousness will prosper and they will not be ashamed.
They will forever be established, unmoved, free and untamed.

Is there Not a Cause?

Is there not reason and a purpose behind the life
that I live?
Is there a vision and aspiration that carries me
through the rain?
Is there a cause for persisting when the walk I walk is
peculiar, uncommon, and often disdained.
Why walk the the road less travelled if there is not an
end in sight?
Why take a step of faith when there is not a hope
empowering the man to persist and fight?
Is there not a cause for what I do? Is there not a
purpose much higher than I?
Is there not a God in heaven charging me to live a
peculiar life, Set apart, Holy, unmoving, godly, not
afraid to die?
What is time, what is a trial if there is not a
reasonable end?
Is there not a cause in choosing a cross, refusing to
live?
Take away the reproach of champions, refuse to
accept what is proclaimed, declared, and said.
Stand in Christ, my Savior, my redeemer, my king,my
rest, my faith, my strength, my morning star, my
friend.
Is there not a cause oh Christian, why have we
settled for the mundane in view of the Holy God.
Take on the whole armor of Christ as He bears the
weight, shield of Faith, Sword of the spirit, with the
gospel our feet shod.

Hold the banner high, may it be terrible in the enemie's sight.

Is there not a cause for life? Stand as Christ holds your stance, stand and fight.

Whatever the giant, the trial, whatever the reproach may be.

Is there not a cause? Look to the Crucified Son lifted high, know faith is real, be set free.

Be no longer established in what is seen, perceived, and heard.

Be moving in faith, simple unadulterated, hanging on every written word.

There is a cause, there is a victory, there is a place in heaven personally set apart for your soul.

Lay not your treasure on this earth, lay treasures in heaven, accept Christ, be whole.

Is there not a cause, little among the thousands, the least of all men, but anointed by God on high.

Is there not a cause, take up your stones, your inadequacies, your doubts, and your despair.

Cast them to the enemy standing before you and witness the fall of the giant as the trouble is taken into God's care.

May the sound of David's courage, the sight of his faith before The giant defying our God's great name, nation and power be the the pattern, the ensample for our own.

Is there not a cause? Is there not an intercessory Savior, a true high priest, a sure and faithful prophet, a King calling you by name from heaven's throne?

Press on, overcome, let Christ work before you, watch your giants fall.

There is a cause, there is an eternal purpose, there is a responsibility to steward a gift of life and walk within a call.

I must Decrease

I must decrease to be exalted and lifted high.
I must decrease to be loving, serving, and cherishing
the friends and family in my life.
I must decrease if I am ever to move forward
through my failures and many faults.
I must decrease as it is my Savior who deserves the
glory, and my redeemer whom I desire to exalt
I must decrease for the world is not enough even if I
had it all to gain.
I must decrease and live as the humble king of kings,
the broken lamb that was slain.

It is the only way of life, it is my desire and utmost
longing within my heart. To decrease is to increase in
Christ, to end and with life anew restart.
We must decrease, we must eliminate the pride and
arrogance festering within. As a cancer it invades, it
hides and grows, it metastasizes into iniquity and sin.
I must decrease and accept the cure, bitter in its
taste but sweet as I become truly well. Into the
darkness I begin, but into the light I am lead and will
eternally dwell.
We must decrease, we must accept the humility of
strength. We must come to terms with faith and let
not reason limit faith's depth, heighth and length.

We are loved with an everlasting love, we are pursued day and night. Do not think in becoming the greatest you will be seen or within God's great sight. For it is in the least of things that my God finds his delight and the least of things can be perfect and right.

Decrease as He increases, Receive truth instead of striving to seek another truth out. For God gives grace to the meek, and strengthens those with simple faith putting aside the selfish and vain doubts. Questions are never declined, they always will have an answer. Decrease before God, I beg of all men please let wisdom have its perfect work.

I decrease, God increases may my life be His laid down boldly, humbly, and reverently before His feet. I decrease, I break, I hunger, my God calls out to me and pleas: Arise and eat. Simply come to Christ, arise and eat.

35073748R00097

Made in the USA
Middletown, DE
18 September 2016